Trinnietta Gets a Chance
Six Families and Their School Choice Experience

by DANIEL MCGROARTY

Foreward by Brother Bob Smith

The Heritage Foundation

The Heritage Foundation
214 Massachusetts Avenue, NE
Washington, DC 20002
800.544.4843
www.heritage.org

Cover photo courtesy of Al Storey
Cover design by Mitzi Hamilton

To My Family:
Jacky, Michele, Erik,
Corey and Andie

Table of Contents

Foreword

by BROTHER BOB SMITH

AFTER ALL THE INTEREST GROUPS have lobbied . . . after all the researchers have published their monographs . . . after all the legislators have passed their measures . . . the full story of school choice in America will be told only when we hear directly from the actual parents and children to whom that movement brought the first breath of hope for a decent education. *Trinnietta Gets a Chance* by Dan McGroarty is a splendid effort to bring us that full story, by examining in detail the struggles and eventual triumphs of six families who find their way to freedom through parental choice in education.

I first met Dan McGroarty in the spring of 1991. I had come to Washington, D.C., as part of a group led by Michael S. Joyce, president and CEO of the Lynde and Harry Bradley Foundation, and Tommy G. Thompson, governor of the state of Wisconsin. Our purpose was to brief the President of the United States and the Secretary of the U.S. Department of Education on the Wisconsin voucher program. One of the people I met during the visit was Dan McGroarty, who then served as one of the President's top speechwriters. I was taken immediately by Dan's sincerity and kindness, but even more by the fact that when we told the Milwaukee story, he truly listened. He would later relate what he heard in his first book, *Break These Chains*.

In his new book, *Trinnietta Gets a Chance: Six Families and Their School Choice Experience*, the national debate on vouchers switches from the White House, the legislative halls, and the courtrooms to the living rooms of everyday Americans. In this poignant book, our focus is put squarely on real people—

people who don't just want shreds of hope, but who cry out for justice. For these economically poor parents, freedom will come only when they are able to escape from poor and failing public schools. For them, and thousands of others like them across the Unites States, freedom will come only when their children at last have access to a high quality education through school choice.

This important book conveys to us the sense of urgency felt by families who are using vouchers. We follow them through their challenges and struggles, but also through their joys and triumphs, as they see their children who were once failing now beginning to experience success. It is clear that McGroarty is one of those rare individuals who, after talking with low-income people and seeing what life is like in economically and educationally deprived America, really "gets it." In so many areas of our country, an entire segment of our population is doomed to a lifetime of mediocrity and dependence. These citizens are trapped in public school systems that provide most with nothing more than expensive day care for the millions of children that fill their halls. These citizens feel hopeless and helpless in the face of a public system that is utterly unresponsive and unaccountable because they have no voice in being able to choose better alternatives for their children's education.

Many opponents of vouchers make a dichotomous argument in order to polarize factions of the public when examining the merits of programs: church versus state walls of separation, public versus private schools, and finally, the "good" folks versus the "bad" folks. The problem with this analysis is that it omits the true principle driving the voucher movement: parental choice. The notion of giving parents choice in schools is not a new or novel idea, at least not for people who have money or the ability to maneuver through a complex and baffling educational system. Only when we seek to expand parental choice to low-income parents does it suddenly raise such specters of dire constitutional, legal, and moral crises for the Republic. McGroarty's book exposes many of the unsavory tactics of choice opponents, which include smear campaigns against individuals supporting or working at private and religious schools, and fear-mongering and outright lying about what really happens in schools that are not run by the government.

Dan McGroarty has captured what all American parents, no matter their economic status, want for their kids—the best. He demonstrates through the stories of these six poor and minority families that their dreams are no different from those of people who are economically safe, and who have had advanced educational opportunities. We see in this book the sacrifices that poor people are willing to make to take their children out of places that threaten them physically and educationally. We walk in the steps of six special families as they journey through the treacherous maze of modern American education. We see the parents who are willing to take on second jobs to pay for private school tuition, so that their children are not treated as mere "numbers." In one particularly poignant story, we see five-year-old Andres get lost and forgotten after his second day at a public school. He is put on the wrong bus, but eventually finds his way home. His desperate and shaken mother initially refuses to send him back to school, but eventually does—after resolving to follow the bus to and from school, to make sure that he is delivered safely.

An important part of the story told here is that vouchers are not some sinister way to fund private and religious schools at the expense of public schools. The schools described in the book did not suddenly become interested in inner-city children only when vouchers appeared, but in fact have quietly been providing them good and successful education for many years. Their principled commitment to the poor and to working in central cities is unassailable. This is particularly apparent when we consider that in many of the religious schools involved, the majority of the students who attend are not even of the faith of the sponsoring school.

The children with whom this book is concerned can be categorized by most measures as "at risk." They are poor, ethnic minority kids often from what sociologists would be quick to call dysfunctional families, students who have special needs and who live in crime-ridden, economically deprived neighborhoods—elements that should inevitably add up to failure by some estimates. The difference in these families is that there are caring parents and guardians who are willing to put it all on the line for their children's futures.

One parent described in the book, Carol Butts, makes this particularly profound observation: "When they attack choice schools, it makes you wonder if they really want communities to work." This really takes us to the heart of the battle over parental choice.

Why is this book by Dan McGroarty so important? It is important because the book speaks with sympathy and respect for real people and real American life. It tells stories of pain and tragedy, but also of hope and new life. I haven't met Kevin Batts or Trinnietta McGrady, Mariano and Marc Alvarez or Roberta Kitchen's five kids, but I feel like I know their stories—because each day I hear stories just like theirs. I work with nearly 800 "at risk" poor and minority children—the same kinds of kids profiled here. These kids fit all the categories that the experts tell us add up to recipes for guaranteed failure. But *Trinnietta Gets a Chance* reassures us that there is hope after all, and that there is a way out of despair. Dan tells a story that will challenge anyone who truly cares about kids and their schools. It should be required reading for educators, legislators, parents, and philanthropists. This book will at times make you angry or drive you to tears. But finally it will make you want to stand and cheer, when we see what great things the human spirit can accomplish when given a chance . . . when given a choice.

BROTHER BOB SMITH, *o.f.m. Capuchin, is president of Messmer High School, an independent Catholic school on Milwaukee's Near North Side. A native of Chicago who worked as a parole officer prior to his involvement in education, Brother Bob served as Messmer's principal from 1987 to 1997, during which he helped "re-establish" the school after it was closed for financial reasons by the Milwaukee archdiocese, and later waged an unsuccessful battle against state authorities to win a place for Messmer High in the fledgling Milwaukee Parental Choice Program. As a result of the expansion of Milwaukee Choice to religious schools in 1998, Messmer now enrolls 333 Choice children in Grades 9 through 12. In response to community demand, Smith has opened Messmer Preparatory Catholic School, a K–8 facility which currently counts 190 Choice children among its total student population of 225. While 70 percent of Messmer High's students come from minority, low-income, single-parent homes, the school has a decade-long graduation rate in the high-90s, and a college-bound graduate rate of 85 percent. Last year, Messmer graduated 66 of its 67 seniors, sending 62 on to two- or four-year colleges, two to military service, and two into the job market.*

Acknowledgements

ONE OF THE THINGS that makes book writing almost bearable is the opportunity it presents to engage intelligent people on an issue of intense interest. First and foremost among the interlocutors I wish to thank is Adam Meyerson of The Heritage Foundation, for sharing my excitement about this project and challenging me to see it to this realization. I also thank Bill Schambra for his advice during the formative stages of this effort, as well as Fritz Steiger and Susan Mitchell for sharing their experience and insight at key points in my research and writing. Of the many people to whom I turned for assistance, advice and information along the way, I wish to single out Clint Bolick, Jay Greene, Patty Hollo, George Mitchell, Nina Rees, Brother Bob Smith, and Teresa Treat. I plan to discharge my debt to all of them by being as responsive in assisting other authors as they were in helping me. Thanks are due also to Elizabeth Schoenfeld for her expert copy editing, to Hunter Campaigne of The Heritage Foundation for all manner of assistance during the research and writing, and to the Lynde and Harry Bradley Foundation, whose generosity made possible my Bradley Fellowship at The Heritage Foundation.

In a project where I felt I was racing deadlines from Day One, my family deserves special thanks. On this project as on all others, my wife Jacqueline's incisive advice kept me on course at critical moments. I also had the pleasure of working professionally with my daughter, Michele Hansen, who proved an able and intrepid research assistant.

Finally, I wish to thank the dozens of parents who do not appear in these pages for taking the time to speak with me about the serious subject of their children's schooling—and of course the families whose stories are chronicled here, whose courage and candor make this book what it is.

~ Daniel McGroarty

Introduction

IN WEST SAN ANTONIO, Juan Alvarez anguishes over the sexual harassment of his son.

On Cleveland's East Side, Roberta Kitchen works to balance her career responsibilities with her role as a single-parent foster mother to five children.

When her oldest daughter doesn't come home to her children, single mother Johnietta McGrady finds herself raising her two grandchildren, along with her own young son and daughter.

In Milwaukee, Carol Butts struggles to find a moral community capable of supporting her family's Muslim faith, while Pilar Gomez copes with the challenge of being a newly single mother of four.

Having raised six children of their own, Leroy Batts and his wife Hattie adopt their grandson after the boy witnesses the murder of his mother.

Different families, different cities, different challenges. Yet there is one thing all of these families have in common.

Each one has children who are benefiting from school choice. Each is using vouchers—funded by public money or private donations—to send its children to private schools they otherwise could not afford.

The six families in this book are linked by a common sense of urgency. Living in cities where the public school graduation rate ranges from 32 percent in Cleveland to 40 percent in San Antonio's Edgewood school district to a "high" of 56 percent in Milwaukee,[1] these parents have little patience for promises of public school improvement, and no time to wait for reform. For these families, vouchers are a life-preserver. As Cleveland's Roberta Kitchen puts it: "Private school is what's giving my children a chance. I have invested too much to let [the public schools] turn my children into something that has a hole in it."

Opponents of school choice say it's wrong to use tax dollars for tuition at religious schools. Their policies would stop Johnietta McGrady, a Baptist, from sending her daughter to the Catholic school where a teacher worked overtime to bring her girl up to grade level. They would stop Carol Butts from sending her four children to the Muslim school where shaping character matters as much as teaching reading, writing, and math.

Opponents say vouchers are wrong because they benefit the "cream of the crop." Under their policies Juan Alvarez would have to keep his son at the public school where a group of boys tried to molest him. Leroy Batts would have to keep his psychologically traumatized grandson in the public school where he was floundering, instead of the Christian academy where for the first time he is learning.

Opponents of choice say voucher children succeed because their parents or guardians are active and engaged, constantly seeking the best education for each of their children. That's right. None of the parents profiled here are strangers at their children's schools. Some, like Johnietta McGrady and Pilar Gomez, are school volunteers; others, like Roberta Kitchen and Carol Butts, have been parent activists at their children's public schools. Given what we know about the positive impact of parental involvement, sound public policy should encourage parental engagement. School choice does.

Surveys tell us that compared with the inner-city average, parents who take advantage of school choice tend themselves to have higher levels of education than parents who elect to keep their children in public school.[2] That is clearly the case with the parents in this book. Roberta Kitchen is working part-time on her master's degree. Leroy Batts, Carol Butts, and Pilar Gomez all graduated from high school in places where a majority of the adult popu-

---

[1.] See State of Wisconsin School Performance Report, Milwaukee, 1998–99 and Cleveland Scholarship Program appellants' brief (*Simmons-Harris, et al. v. Zelman, et al.*, March 31, 2000), p. 20. According to Robert Aguirre, managing director of CEO Horizon, the dropout rate for Hispanics in the Edgewood district, an area of San Antonio that is 98 percent Hispanic, is 60 percent (CEO America Conference, Grand Rapids, Michigan, May 17, 2000).

lation dropped out. Even the exceptions prove the rule: After leaving school in their teens, Juan Alvarez and Johnietta McGrady went back to school as adults to earn their GEDs. In each case, the signal sent by parents profiled here is that education is worth working for: A critical lesson for children regardless of race or income level.

As the stories in this book make clear, vouchers are not a panacea. School choice, for instance, will not turn all students into scholars. Johnietta McGrady's daughter Trinnietta has not become a stellar student in parochial school. She has, however, progressed from being a less-than-average student to an average student, an important improvement, given that the achievement scores of inner-city public school students typically *decline* one to two points each year they are in school. What's more, seven-year-old Trinnietta regularly helps her eight-year-old nephew, a public school student, with his lessons during the McGrady homework hour.

Nor can school choice insulate parents from making choices they regret. As Roberta Kitchen observes of her own odyssey through public and private schools, "Just because a school is private doesn't mean it's perfect." In fact, in the quest to find the right school for each child, some of the families have transferred their children from *private* schools to *public* schools—in the case of Pilar Gomez's oldest daughter, three times. The advantage of choice is that when parents are unhappy with a school, they can send their child elsewhere.

[2.] However, "random assignment" studies of Milwaukee's Parental Choice program as well as privately funded school choice programs in Dayton, Ohio, Washington, D.C., and New York City show that vouchers improve student achievement even when one controls for parents' educational backgrounds.

See, for instance, Jay P. Greene, Paul E. Peterson and Jiangtao Du's "Effectiveness of School Choice: The Milwaukee Experiment," Harvard Program on Education Policy and Governance, March 1997, where the authors observe in "Controlling for Family Background," Table 4: "To explore whether [differences in family background] contaminate our results [which showed choice students, after four years in the program, scoring 10.7 points higher in math and 5.8 points higher in reading compared with the control group], Table 4 reports the results of a fixed effects analysis that takes into account gender, mother's education, parents' marital status, income, education expectations and time spent with the child . . . . The number of cases available for analysis is . . . considerably reduced and the point estimates are less reliable. Nevertheless, all point estimates are positive and six of the eight are actually larger than those reported in the main analysis."

The parents profiled here are not anti-public school; they have simply come to the conclusion that the public school to which their child has been assigned is not the right choice at the right time for that child. Choice gives them the chance to find the school that *is* right.

Pilar Gomez. Carol Butts. Johnietta McGrady. Roberta Kitchen. Leroy Batts. Juan Alvarez. None of these names appear in the op-ed sections of America's newspapers, nor on the policy panels of the country's innumerable conferences on education reform. Yet each offers a perspective we've missed on a policy of critical importance to the state of our schools.

The pages that follow offer a study in six parts of the most passionately argued-about school reform ever in the annals of American education, from voices seldom heard in the voucher debate—the parents who have chosen choice for their children.

Chapter One

MILWAUKEE

MILWAUKEE

IN THE UNRELENTING RHETORICAL WAR over the issue of vouchers, Milwaukee, Wisconsin is ground zero: the first, and for five years, the only publicly funded private school choice program. Dating back to a voucher proposal advanced by Milton Friedman in 1955, school choice had been a perennial in the public education reform debate; yet no jurisdiction at any level of government had implemented a choice program until March 1990, when the Wisconsin state legislature passed the ground-breaking Milwaukee Parental Choice Program as part of an omnibus budget act.

Parental Choice was the brainchild of former welfare-mother-turned-state-legislator Polly Williams, a Democrat representing Milwaukee's predominantly African-American Near North Side. Williams pushed the proposal through the legislature by forging a strange-bedfellow coalition linking a small core of otherwise liberal Democrats, most of them African-American, all united by a despair over the state of public urban education, and a larger bloc of white, Republican legislators from suburban and smalltown Wisconsin who were philosophically inclined toward the concept of school choice.

As initially enacted, Milwaukee's Parental Choice Program was relatively modest in scope. The program was confined to just 1 percent of the Milwaukee Public Schools' student population, then about 1,000 students, and the choice of schools was limited to the city's non-religious, "community" schools. Each voucher was valued at $2,500, the state's share of per-pupil expenditure, and approximately half of what public schools spent per child; choice schools would have to agree to accept the voucher as payment in full, with no ability to charge parents additional tuition. Choice schools were denied the ability to reject a voucher student, and children were awarded vouchers through a lottery, to ensure impartiality and to deal with demand in excess of the 1,000 slots. Of the two dozen community schools in Milwaukee, just six stepped forward to participate in the program, none of them high schools; Milwaukee's more than 80 religious schools were not allowed to participate.

Modest in scope or no, the Parental Choice Program was perceived by the public education establishment as a threat to the system. The firestorm was immediate. Wisconsin's state superintendent of public instruction, Herbert Grover, who was designated by law to administer the new program, pronounced Milwaukee Choice "fundamentally flawed and very possibly unconstitutional,"[1] and issued repeated public invitations to associations in the public education establishment to sue to stop the Milwaukee experiment before it began. Grover got his wish; within a month, Milwaukee's NAACP, joined by Wisconsin's two main public teachers unions and a variety of administrative organizations, brought suit. Parental Choice's odyssey through the legal system had begun. The program was upheld in trial court weeks before the 1990–91 school year was to begin; in late August, 341 voucher students from low-income Milwaukee families attended a handful of private, non-religious schools across the city. Before the first semester was over, however, a state appeals court ruled the program unconstitutional on a procedural point related to the program's passage as part of an omnibus budget. For the next sixteen months, Parental Choice existed under a constitutional cloud, until March 1992, when the Wisconsin Supreme Court found the program constitutional.

Milwaukee took the choice debate to the next level in the summer of 1995, when the Wisconsin legislature expanded the program to allow students to take their vouchers to Milwaukee's religious schools as well. In the third

---

[1] "Top Educator Calls Choice Plan 'Flawed,'" *Milwaukee Sentinel,* June 2, 1990.

week of August 1995, more than 1,000 students from low-income Milwaukee families became the first ever to use a publicly funded voucher to attend the religious school of their choice. On August 21, however, the Wisconsin Supreme Court handed down an injunction halting the expanded Choice program until its constitutionality was decided. Donors to Milwaukee's privately funded voucher program, PAVE (Partners Advancing Values in Education), rushed in to provide sufficient funds to pay half-tuition for the stranded voucher students; the expanded Choice program remained in legal limbo, however, for nearly three years, until the Wisconsin Supreme Court upheld the program's constitutionality in June 1998. In the fall of 1998, 6,200 Milwaukee children used vouchers to attend more than 90 private schools across the city, including Protestant, Catholic, Muslim and Jewish schools.

Even as the long-delayed expanded choice program took effect, anti-voucher forces made good on their oft-repeated threat to use every legal means possible to kill Milwaukee choice, appealing the Wisconsin ruling to the U.S. Supreme Court. On November 8, 1998, the U.S. high court refused to hear the Wisconsin appeal, effectively allowing the Wisconsin ruling to stand, and the expanded Milwaukee Parental Choice Program to exist.

Nevertheless, the education establishment's assault on Milwaukee Choice continues. In 1999, People for the American Way and Milwaukee's NAACP conducted a "sting operation" against Milwaukee Parental Choice, encouraging members to pose as parents in an attempt to draw religious choice schools into program violations. PFAW and the NAACP have now petitioned Wisconsin's Department of Public Instruction to investigate alleged infractions. The legislative and legal battles may be over, but Milwaukee's voucher wars rage on.

The public education establishment may not have made its peace with the Parental Choice Program, but many other public figures in Milwaukee have embraced the voucher cause. The city's mayor, John O. Norquist, has been an enthusiastic school choice supporter from the first, in the face of continued opposition from fellow Democrats. In 1999, Wisconsin's teacher unions vowed to make a school board election a referendum on the parental choice program; every union-endorsed candidate lost, giving voucher supporters a solid majority on the Milwaukee School Board. In the aftermath of the school board elections, Milwaukee Public Schools' new superintendent publicly appeared with the city's Catholic archbishop, promising collaboration on school programs[2] and acknowledging that he had a "moral obligation to question whether some students could be better served than they are now in public schools, and that private school choice might offer that opportunity."[3]

Today, ten years after 341 children reported to seven inner-city schools, more than 10,000 students use vouchers to attend more than 100 schools across Milwaukee. Yet the impact of Parental Choice is not limited to the students using vouchers. Howard L. Fuller, former Milwaukee Public School superintendent and school choice advocate, argues that private school choice is sparking public school change, as the city's public education system comes to grips with the need to compete for students who now have other educational options.[4]

---

[2] "Archdiocese, District Agree to Work Together," *Milwaukee Journal Sentinel,* June 10, 1999.

[3] "Tide First Turned When Justice Upheld Choice," *Milwaukee Journal Sentinel,* June 10, 1999.

[4] For a detailed account of Fuller's argument, see Policy Postscript below, p. 136ff.

Milwaukee Parental Choice Program
FIRST YEAR IN OPERATION: 1990–91

Eligibility:
- 175% of federal poverty level
- Resident of the city of Milwaukee
- Students selected by lottery, if more applicants than slots available

Value of voucher:
- $5,106 for 1999–2000 year

Current participation:
- 9,638 students at 104 schools for the 2000–2001 year
- Program capped at 15% of Milwaukee's public school system enrollment

Pilar Gomez says goodbye to her youngest son, Tomas, as Andres and Bianca greet Prince of Peace Principal Donna Schmidt.

PILAR GOMEZ

*"[Y]ou have to go in and get every bit of
information you can. We ask questions about
every other decision we make in life. I mean,
I'll ask how good a car is, but not a teacher?"*

IT WAS FRIDAY, AUGUST 21, 1995. Pilar Gomez remembers the first
phone call coming not long before noon, about half an hour after she had
learned that the Wisconsin Supreme Court had issued a one-sentence injunction halting the expansion of the Milwaukee Parental Choice Program to religious schools. Pilar, who until the end of the previous school year had been a
parent organizer with a group called Parents for School Choice, was used to
fielding parent inquiries of all sorts. But the mother on the other end of the
phone that day was distraught. "She wanted to know, could they do that,"
Pilar recalls, "could they just stop the [Milwaukee Parental Choice] program,
now that the school year had already started?" And in fact, across Milwaukee, about 1,000 students had already reported to fourteen religious schools
that had begun the school year.

"She had so many questions," Pilar remembers. "Word was spreading at
the schools that the injunction had been handed down. No one knew what to
do, and all kinds of things were flying around."

Pilar got off the phone with the woman, and the phone rang immediately.
It was another parent. She answered over three dozen calls in the next four
hours. "I was telling all these parents, don't worry," remembers Pilar. "It will

all get worked out. Keep sending your kids to school. And then all of a sudden, the calls stopped and the house was quiet, and it started to sink in. I just felt so bad. And I thought, what am I going to tell Bianca and Andres?"

Pilar's two grade school children were scheduled to start school the next Monday at St. Lawrence, a Catholic school about two blocks from Pilar's home, their tuition to be paid in full by a Milwaukee choice voucher. Now the court was stopping them.

"I didn't know what to tell my kids," recalls Pilar. "Andres and Bianca were so excited, talking about school and seeing all their friends there. I was just sick. All weekend, I couldn't sleep, I couldn't eat," Pilar continues. "On Monday, we got ready for school. My eyes kept tearing up, so I put on sunglasses. I was thinking about how much I had looked forward to walking them to school," Pilar continues, "and I just couldn't stop wondering how long it was going to be before we had to pull them out of St. Lawrence."

Pilar packed Tomas, her toddler, into his stroller, "and I said to Bianca and her brother, okay, 'Let's skip and let's sing.' It's only a short walk, so I tried to keep it light all the way there. But when I got to the school, I could see the parents there, waiting out front. Some were crying. And they started calling over, 'Pilar, can you come here?' So I told the kids, 'Okay, find your friends and go play.'"

Pilar stood on the school steps for the next hour and a half, answering questions, writing her phone number on scraps of paper, "telling [parents] to call me, and I would give them all the information I had."

Sister Joan, the principal at St. Lawrence, "was handing out forms for a diocesan grant," recalls Pilar. "People were talking about PAVE [Partners Advancing Values in Education, the large, privately funded voucher organization active in Milwaukee since 1992] coming in with assistance, but that was going to be half-tuition," says Pilar, leaving the low-income parents served by the Milwaukee choice program to come up with the remaining $400 per child. "The diocesan grant was $30—*for the year*. It was good to have help, but...."

Pilar and her husband Juan received PAVE half-tuition grants for Bianca and Andres, and made their portion of the first monthly payment to St.

Lawrence. Several weeks into September, however, with the prospect of regular payments looming, they looked at the hard facts. Two shares of tuition was more than the family budget could bear. "Our question was: Okay, which one of our kids do we keep [at St. Lawrence], and which one do we move back?"

"It came down to, who needed more specialized attention?" recalls Pilar. "And that was definitely Andres. Bianca, we knew, could survive. And Doerfler," Bianca's old school, "was one of the better MPS schools, so we were confident she could make it work there."

"But it was hard, moving your kids around like that, splitting them up. It was the kind of thing a lot of parents were dealing with. I mean, no one liked it, but it was just what we had to do."

• • •

PILAR GOMEZ WAS BORN and raised in Milwaukee, and has lived her entire life in a two-and-a-half-mile radius from the North Side house she grew up in to the home she's buying today, on Milwaukee's heavily Hispanic South Side. "My parents still live over on 20th Street, in St. Michael's parish. It's predominantly an African-American neighborhood now. They live in the duplex my grandparents owned."

Pilar graduated from Milwaukee Tech, an MPS high school. A year later, Pilar had a baby, her daughter Leigha. "Never went to college," says Pilar. "While I was in high school, I started work as a dental assistant. And then when I had my daughter, I worked part-time," says Pilar. "I was living at home. I needed health insurance, and I didn't have that with part-time work. So I looked into what I could do to get insurance, and the only thing was to quit and go on welfare. Crazy, isn't it?"

"I decided that wasn't for me, and so I started thinking, what else can I do? I got a job as a cosmetics dealer," says Pilar, who found it easier to balance the odd hours of sales work around her daughter's needs. "I was doing all right, keeping my head above water."

In 1984, Pilar met Juan Gonzalez. "Three weeks after we met, we were engaged," recalls Pilar, now divorced from her husband. "We got married one year to the day we met." Juan Gonzalez, born in Mexico, worked in a Milwaukee tannery, about eight blocks from their home. "My husband really wanted me to stay home," says Pilar. "And I did. But if you know me, I'm not really the stay-at-home mom type."

In 1984, before she met Juan, Pilar had taken the Post Office employment exam. "They never called me. You were covered by the same exam for three years, and just before the time ran out, they called with a job." Pilar took it.

"I was what they call a letter sorting machine operator, running all that high tech, automated-type equipment."

I ask Pilar how long she worked there. "Oh God, too long. Way too long. I started in 1987 and worked there five years. It was a really bad experience. I mean, they timed you when you went to the bathroom."

"They couldn't pay me enough to stay at the Post Office, seriously. It's a high stress job," says Pilar. "Stressful in the sense that the work was easy to do, but the management staff, the administrative rules were so unbearable, so when you hear about the term being postal, they mean that."

Five years after she took the job, Pilar quit the Post Office. "I knew I wouldn't find a job that paid as much as the Post Office did, but it got to be a matter of my own dignity. If you're a good worker, you can't work in that environment."

If Pilar was no longer drawing a paycheck, it did not mean she was done working. "About a year before, I started doing work—not for pay, just as a volunteer—with an organization called the Fair Lending Coalition," recalls Pilar. "It's an advocacy group that tries to ensure that our CRAs [the Community Reinvestment Act] are followed, and there's no lending discrimination. I became part of an oversight group. I oversaw the banks of Milwaukee, lending practices, the CRA ratings, things like that."

"After Fair Lending, I was what they call a targeted investment neighborhood coordinator. I was advocating for a small eight-to-ten-square block area in a poverty-stricken neighborhood, just outside my neighborhood, about four blocks away. My job was trying to make sure that homeowners would get the assistance they needed to qualify for block grants, homeowner and home improvement loans at a very low rate, things like that."

"We actually had to make a plan, you know, with a time line and a certain time frame, to get the streets repaved here, we have to get street lights installed here," Pilar continues. "Anything that would enhance the quality of the neighborhood. That included credit and budgeting counseling, and so during this time I actually also became a home ownership counselor." In 1994, Pilar and Juan Gonzalez became homeowners themselves, buying a house on South 28th Street.

"That was around the time we moved my oldest daughter Leigha to St. Lawrence," for her eighth grade year. "I was up at the school a lot, volunteering for this and that. And I started doing delegate liaison work between three Catholic churches and their schools. I was still doing that in 1995, when a fellow from a group called Parents for School Choice came around to the schools looking for people that wanted to take a job as parent organizer. I ended up going to an interview, and I got the job."

"My mom was at my house, babysitting for me, and I came in all excited and told her what I'd be doing. And she said, 'That's great, Pilar. What are they going to pay you?' And I was so embarrassed. I hadn't asked. And I had to work up my nerve to call back and ask what the pay was."

"When I find something I believe in doing," says Pilar, "you know, the pay is almost—it doesn't matter."

• • •

LONG BEFORE PILAR GOMEZ was a parent organizer she was a parent, and long before programs like Milwaukee Parental Choice or PAVE existed, Pilar was grappling with the challenges of educating a child.

Leigha Gomez, Pilar's oldest daughter, is now nineteen, and a high school graduate. "Thank goodness," adds Pilar. "Leigha graduated last June [1999] from Grand Avenue," an alternative high school in the Milwaukee Public School system. "It was a good experience for her. She was always a 'Gifted and Talented' girl, extremely intelligent. Her problem was that school, whether it's public or private, never seemed to challenge her."

"Most of the time, she coasted through," Pilar recalls. "The only time we saw Leigha's grades go down was when she was at Pius," the Catholic high school Leigha attended for two years before tranferring and graduating from Grand. "At Pius, they were telling me, 'She knows what she's doing, we know she knows what she's doing, but she's not putting herself into it.'"

"With Leigha, that's the way it was all the way through."

"I started her off in Catholic school," Pilar recalls, "at St. Matthew," three blocks from home. It was 1985; Pilar and her mother paid Leigha's $650 a year tuition. "That was fine, until Leigha was in the second grade, and her teacher told me, 'We have a very, very smart kid here. I don't think we're going to be able to address her needs here.'"

The suggestion surprised Pilar. "As a product of the public schools myself, and as a first-time mom, it had just always been my experience that a better education was available in private school. It was a shock to hear Leigha's teacher talking about moving her to a public school that could help her more."

Leigha's teacher recommended a Gifted and Talented program at MPS's Dover Elementary School. "She said, the only way she could get into it is if somebody wrote her a letter of recommendation and she said, 'I'm willing to write that letter for her.' But I was leery of sending Leigha to the public schools, so I said, if you can't address her needs, let me go to another Catholic school around here and see if they could. Her teacher said, 'Okay, do that, and have the principal or the teacher call me and we can try to make it work.'"

Pilar also raised the possibility of advancing Leigha a grade. "But they said the archdiocese really didn't like doing that, because academically, she might be able to do it, but socially, she might not fit in. It might not show up when she's in fourth grade but maybe fifth or sixth grade it would show up and then it would be too late for them to undo it."

"Well, all the other Catholic schools I spoke to really couldn't come up with anything the teacher and I both felt comfortable with, so I said, okay. Let's put her in public school. And I did get her in the Gifted and Talented program at Dover."

Academically, Pilar believes Dover served Leigha well. "It was a good experience in the classroom. And the school was culturally diverse, which was good. Gifted and Talented is really like a school within a school, so Leigha was always in small classes, with individual attention."

Dover ended with fifth grade; Pilar enrolled her daughter at Lincoln Middle School in the MPS. "In class, Leigha was able to breeze by. I mean, she had straight A's there," says Pilar. Still, what she learned at a school conference concerned her. "Leigha had an A in this class, but I found she had completed just three of the assignments, and there were eight. And I said to the teacher, 'Oh my God, you can't allow this. She's not learning. She's not deserving the grade.'"

"I told the teacher, I want Leigha to realize there are consequences to her actions," Pilar continues, "and if she's getting an A for not doing anything, that's not what Leigha needs to learn."

Leigha was also having problems adjusting to middle school life outside the classroom. "You know, in sixth grade you're impressionable," says Pilar. "And Leigha was used to being in a smaller school, and of course the Gifted and Talented program is even smaller in terms of the other children she's with all day."

"And she goes from there to this junior high where they've got lockers and they're changing classes and socially it just took a toll on her. She didn't know how to deal with it."

Leigha finished the year at Lincoln, but Pilar made the decision to transfer her daughter yet again. "I took her to St. Lawrence School. I explained to the principal there, I said, you know, she's not really a behavioral problem. She's got that book-smart smart-alecky type attitude. And I was worried that the Catholic school was going to say, 'No way. We don't want her impressing this type of attitude on the kids here.'"

"But Sister Joan," St. Lawrence's principal, "said, 'I can see your daughter has lots of qualities in her, and although she may not really want to be here, we'll try to work with her.'"

St. Lawrence seemed the right choice. "Leigha liked it, she liked it a lot. I saw her attitude change. She wanted to do the work and things like that. I thought, oh good, this is just what she needs." Then Leigha became ill, and was twice hospitalized for what doctors said was mononucleosis and hepatitis. Leigha "missed a good two months' worth of school with this illness," Pilar remembers. "The principal stayed after school and worked with me on her homework, and tried to catch her up. She said, 'You're going to graduate.' And she did."

Leigha was ready to begin high school, but during her bouts of illness had missed the entry exams for Catholic schools. "So we looked into sending her to Riverside," a sought-after high school in the MPS system. "This was my thinking," says Pilar. "When I took her to Riverside, I had two cousins of mine attending school, boys who were Gifted and Talented. So, I said, okay, since they're getting their needs met, let's try it." Pilar was impressed that students at Riverside could even take college courses once they reached a certain level.

Pilar saw almost immediately that Leigha was falling into her old ways at Riverside. "I could see that she wasn't being challenged like I hoped she would. I spoke to a few of her teachers and they said, well she knows her work. I was hoping she would do a little bit more, go that extra distance. But she did what she had to do and that was it. I felt like I was the bad guy, always on her, 'come on, come on, don't just do a one-page report, do two.' Leigha didn't want to be bothered. She said, 'Mom, they only asked for a one-pager, all the other kids only do one page.' I felt like I was always on her."

Pilar didn't wait to see a turnaround. She simply made arrangements to transfer Leigha to Pope Pius XI, a Catholic high school on Milwaukee's South Side, for her sophomore year. At Pius, "they told me when she's a junior, with special consideration, depending on her grades and attendance, she can be here half days and then go to work half day, in a related field that she wants to be in," recalls Pilar. "They only offered that for seniors, but because of her special needs, they said perhaps they would do that for her."

With a course load heavy with advanced classes, Leigha's sophomore year went reasonably well. Junior year, however, Leigha slumped. "It was the same story. Her junior year, she lost interest and her grades started going down," says Pilar. "I think she took advantage of the situation, didn't apply herself as well as she could have. And socially she was having some problems there. All the schools she had attended before were very diverse, even the public schools, and Pius had a group of girls that were really prominent who came from much more upscale families."

"Leigha finally came to a point where she came home one day and said, 'Mom, I'm not happy.' Because, you know, we were poor—let's face it," says Pilar. "Leigha would go to school and she would say, 'These kids look me up and down and judge me based on the kind of shoes I'm wearing. I can't take that any more.' I told her, you'll have to deal with different kinds of people all your life," recalls Pilar, "maybe you can just deal with these people now."

"But she didn't want to be there, she didn't want to apply herself," says Pilar. For the first time, Leigha began to exhibit some behavioral problems at school. "It was a lose-lose situation, so we pulled her out."

Pilar talked to a family member who taught in the MPS system, looking for a school that might be right for Leigha. "That's how I heard about Grand Avenue," recalls Gomez of the alternative high school run by MPS. Grand was closer to Pilar's house, just across the viaduct separating south side from north side Milwaukee. "And the school is on the Marquette campus," says Pilar, "so it seemed like the right kind of atmosphere for Leigha."

"So we enrolled Leigha there. She liked it. She liked it right away," says Pilar Gomez, "and that's the school she graduated from."

• • •

I TALK TO PILAR ABOUT THE PROCESS that took her oldest daughter to six schools in twelve years, and three times involved a transfer from private to public schools. "Leigha was my first. Dealing with her education taught me to pay a little bit more attention to my children's individual needs and to act on whatever concerns about a school I had early on, not to wait to see how things might change. I didn't want to have any more regrets."

"Seeing how things went with Leigha made me be more active, more participatory, more attentive to Andres's special needs, because there's just no way I can afford to get anything wrong educationally for him. And for Bianca, never to let her coast, and always to make sure she's challenged at school."

With six and eight years' difference between Leigha and Pilar's second and third children, Pilar had more experience to bring to bear on Andres's and Bianca's education. And with Andres and Bianca coming of school age in the early and mid-90s, Milwaukee's Parental Choice Program gave Pilar Gomez more educational options.

"I started Andres at Dover, where Leigha was. Then when Leigha went up to middle school, we put Andres in Zablocki," an MPS elementary school not far from Pilar's home. With MPS committed through its desegregation agreement to bus children to enhance racial balance, Gomez had unusual freedom to transfer her children wherever an Hispanic child improved the racial mix. "There was a change of principals at the time that Leigha was leaving Dover and I really wasn't real sure about the direction that school was going," recalls Pilar. "Rather than deal with that uncertainty, I wanted to go somewhere where it was very consistent. And Zablocki was a good school."

In 1995, the summer after Andres's second grade year, the Wisconsin legislature expanded the Milwaukee Parental Choice Program from the limited number of non-religious, "community" schools to all religious schools within the city of Milwaukee. Pilar, following every move in the legislative battle, had the paperwork done for vouchers for Andres and Bianca "before the ink was dry." It was that August that Pilar enrolled both children at St. Lawrence, only to have to remove Bianca when the court injunction pulled the choice program out from under her.

"It was even before we moved Bianca back," Pilar recalls. "Andres's teacher called me in, and said he had a problem. She said, 'I'm not a professional, but I want you to know that I think that he has attention deficit disorder. I don't think he's hyperactive, but he definitely has difficulty holding attention for a long time.'"

The teacher advised Pilar to have Andres "M-teamed," the bureaucratic phrase of art for the battery of diagnostic tests administered by the MPS system to determine learning disability and special needs. "And I refused that. I was aware of other parents who had had their children tested in MPS, and I didn't see any significant change in how their children were treated, or how they were being provided for. They were just labeled."

"Here they were getting more money for those labeled kids, and weren't providing anything you could see. For the extra $7,000 you would think they would really have something going here for those kids, but they didn't. I didn't want Andres labeled. I figured, okay, he's had a challenge already, a mark against him, I don't want that to carry on with his educational career."

"Maybe it was a bad judgment on my part, I still think not, but I thought there were other ways to help him."

After Andres struggled through a second year at St. Lawrence, Pilar realized a change was in order. "They could not meet his needs," says Pilar. "I took him back to Doerfler, his old public school. We had him studied by a private psychologist who did confirm he was ADD. And Doerfler said, well, you could have him M-teamed, too. He'll receive more assistance. I said, 'Tell me how he would receive more assistance,'" says Pilar. "'Guarantee that to me, and then I will do that.' They couldn't."

"We saw a change with the Ritalin," says Pilar. "A negative change. He actually started beginning behavioral problems where he didn't have them before. At the risk of sounding like a boastful parent, Andres was like the ideal child. I mean, he is such a good boy. Anything I say, he listens. He just doesn't always absorb it and hold it in."

"All of a sudden, I would ask him something simple like, 'Could you get your sister a glass of water,' and he said, 'No way, tell her to get it herself.' Had that come from one of my other children, I might not have raised an eyebrow, but when he said it, I was shocked. This was happening on a regular basis. So I called the doctor and said, 'What happens if I just stop giving this to him? Is there going to be any adverse reaction? Do I have to worry about anything?' He said, 'No. Once you stop giving it to him, in a few hours it's totally out of him.' I said, 'Fine, I'm stopping it.'" Today, Andres takes herbal medicines that Pilar believes benefit him. His behavior problems vanished when he stopped taking Ritalin.

Pilar has a positive view of Andres's experience at Doerfler. "Andres had really excellent teachers at Doerfler," says Pilar. "Mrs. Taylor for fifth grade, and Miss Richardson and Mr. Edler for sixth. But when he was going to go on to middle school, that was the summer we had a real medical scare with him. We had to have him cancer screened. He was negative. I just kept thinking about how he'd get lost at the middle school. It was so much bigger. And I just wanted a way to keep him closer to home."

The way came in June 1998, when Wisconsin's Supreme Court upheld the constitutionality of the expanded Parental Choice Program. Pilar weighed her options; "I kept thinking about St. Lawrence, and how far Andres had come since he left there." Pilar decided to use a voucher to send Andres to St. Lawrence for seventh grade.

• • •

IF ANDRES PRESENTED PILAR the challenge of meeting a child's special needs, Bianca posed a different challenge, one that reminded Pilar of her experience with Leigha.

Pilar's plan had been to move Bianca in tandem with Andres, starting her in four-year-old kindergarten at Zablocki, and moving her for five-year-old kindergarten to Doerfler. "Otherwise it was like I would have kids everywhere."

Yet Pilar saw signs that Doerfler might not be the right place for Bianca. "She struggled while she was there," recalls Pilar. "Even though it was kindergarten, she was very aware. Bianca is a very attuned-type person, she knew what works for her and what didn't, even at that young age. She would come home and say, 'Mom, you know, I don't like just going to school and playing games.' She can articulate very well, and she did even then."

"So how do you say to a kid who's five years old that kids aren't all on the same level and the teacher can't just focus on some kids more than others? So I said, okay, I think we need to start looking at other options for her. And that meant probably putting her in a private school."

It was 1995, the year the Milwaukee choice program expanded, and Bianca spent a brief three weeks at St. Lawrence Catholic School before the injunction forced Pilar and her husband to re-enroll Bianca at her old public school.

Back at Doerfler, Bianca struggled. "She just couldn't do it. I could see it right away," Pilar recalls. "Her teacher was an exceptional teacher on top of that, but even with that, she just could not adjust."

"So I talked it over with my husband. I said, you know, I think we have to find a way to keep her in private school for her educational career, because I don't think she can function well in that setting. Maybe when she gets older and she adjusts socially, public school would be great. But not now."

For the next two years, Pilar and Juan struggled financially to enroll both Bianca and Andres at St. Lawrence, relying on private PAVE grants for half the tuition. At one point, when the family could not keep up their payments, an anonymous donor stepped forward to cover a shortfall.

I ask Pilar what she's learned as a result of piloting four children through eighteen schools, public and private. "It's a fight to find the right school, and the right school for one [child] may not be the right school for the others," says Pilar. "That's what I've learned. So you have to go in and get every bit of information you can. We ask questions about every other decision we make in life. I mean, I'll ask how good a car is, but not a teacher?"

Today, all three of Pilar's school-age children are enrolled at Prince of Peace/Principe de Paz, the new school formed in 1999 when St. Matthew and St. Lawrence schools merged for financial reasons, their total $1,800 tuition covered by vouchers provided through the expanded Parental Choice program. Pilar's youngest son, Tomas, has just finished first grade at Prince of Peace. Says Pilar: "That's where I plan to keep him."

• • •

PILAR WANTS A STRONG CULTURE and community in her children's schools. "When I was growing up," Pilar relates, "we had a strong sense of community. And the school was the cornerstone, with Friday fish fries, what have you. In MPS, with all the moving around, that's not possible. But at Prince of Peace, it's happening now."

"Andres now knows the boy down the block, who's lived there six years, but they went to different schools and they hadn't met," continues Pilar. "Now he's got a neighborhood friend, a school friend. And that's meaningful to me."

As for the educational experience she seeks for her children, Pilar explains how two different sets of considerations led her to the same school for Bianca and Andres. "Bianca is headstrong," says Pilar. "She needs the additional discipline. When she was in MPS, there were mornings when she had headaches, her stomach hurt, she didn't want to go to school," Pilar recalls. "Now, at night, I don't have to remind her as much to get her homework done. And in the morning, she's ready to leave the house before I am. It's not so much that you see it in her grades, but there's been a big change in attitude, in the willingness to go to school, and her desire to learn."

"Andres," says Pilar, "is a little bit different. At MPS, he had some really good teachers the last two years, but even so, they gave him his assignment, and said 'Do your best.' That's it. There weren't many expectations placed upon a child like Andres to really push himself."

"At Prince of Peace, the expectations are much higher," notes Pilar, even for special needs children like her son. "Andres knows they want quality work. They don't expect him to do more than he has ability to do; but they do expect him to do as much as he can. They tell him, 'Set goals for yourself. If you want a B, what's your plan to get there?'"

"Sometimes with his disabilities, I've let [Andres] use me as a crutch," admits Pilar. "I know that. That's why what's happening at Prince of Peace is so important. I have a great deal of confidence that this school reinforces moral values, but also the educational strengths that I want for [Andres]."

"They catch him quicker when he's not paying attention," says Pilar, recalling a recent instance where the school called her to report that Andres had been talking in class. "Andres is struggling right now, his grades are not the best. Prince of Peace doesn't do social promotions. I think a few times that did happen [to Andres] in MPS. I got a letter last week with a box checked that said, 'we highly recommend that your child enroll in the summer enrichment sessions.' And we'll do that with Andres," Pilar continues. "But there was also a box that was not checked, that said 'your child's advancing to the next grade is conditioned on attending the summer enrichment sessions.' So Andres is not at that point, but we've got to watch with him."

Even with his classroom difficulties, however, Pilar sees a change in her older son's attitude toward school. "He's confident he can do the work. The teachers sent home an extra set of textbooks for tutoring," says Pilar, "and he's had some high 80s on a few projects and tests lately." Pilar, hoping to build on Andres's sense of accomplishment, recalls a breakthrough in her son's first year at Prince of Peace.

"Andres got totally involved in a project on the Aztec culture. While he was working on it, he kept asking me if we could get some Aztec artifacts, so finally we went to an import store and I bought him a ceremonial Aztec mask. In the store, he started telling me all about it: How it was used in the rituals, what priest wore it, and so on," recalls Pilar. "I was surprised by that."

"Then he was calling family members for information. My family has roots tracing back to the Aztecs, and Andres was talking to my father about stories he remembered as a child," marvels Pilar. "Andres was into it."

"So finally, he brought his project home, and he said, "Mom, I got an A+,'" Pilar recalls. "He had never had an A+ or even an A before."

"Well, I started crying. I just couldn't talk. He was so proud. So I hugged him and I said, 'Go get in the car, we've got to go show Grandma and Grandpa.'"

"We keep that project out where we can see it," says Pilar. "So Andres has some reminder of what he can do, what he's capable of."

• • •

I ASK PILAR ABOUT THE IMPULSE behind her activism, and its relationship to her concerns as a parent. "The people I deal with, the connection is that you're a parent, like they're a parent. You put your own experience into what you do. Take the way people in Milwaukee feel about busing, and not wanting their kids bused an hour and a half each way all over town," says Pilar. "That's a big reason people are for choice, and just from a safety standpoint, I can see that."

"When my son Andres was just about to start school, I was at his school and I told the principal, 'What I'm nervous about is my son being so young and having such a long bus ride.'

"The first day of school came, and Andres went," recalls Pilar. "No problem. So now it's the second day, and the day's over, and the bus pulls up and I'm waiting for Andres to get off, and he's not getting off."

"And I remember I heard something, and I turned for a minute, and all of a sudden the bus takes off. I said, 'Wait a minute.' I'm yelling, 'The bus hasn't stopped.'"

"Now, we live in a corner house, and about eight MPS buses have their bus stops right across the street from our front window, including Andres's bus. So I run back into my house now, and I call the bus number, and say, 'Could you ask the bus driver, he's got to be a few blocks from my house, ask him to stop back because he didn't let my son off the bus.' So they call the bus and the guy said, 'Well, he stopped, but your son didn't get off the bus because your son wasn't on the bus.'"

"And I said, 'No. He must mean he's sleeping,'" Pilar continues. "You know I was cold all over all of the sudden. He said, 'The bus driver pulled over. He's looking for your son. Your son is not on that bus.'"

"So I said, then he's crying at the school right now, and here I am on the phone. So I called the school and I said, is my son in your office there? And they said, no we don't have any kids in the office. So, I said, okay, the teacher's probably got him, something like that. The school's about three miles from our house. That's far enough, especially for a five-year-old. If it had been three blocks, my five-year-old wouldn't have known the difference."

"So I'm talking to the principal, and he says, 'Well, don't hang up, Mrs. Gonzalez,' and I could hear him talking to the bus company on another phone. And he came back on and said, 'He's on somebody's bus. They're going to put an all-page out to all the buses saying that if they've got a lost boy they should call in.'"

"Now, my husband walks in the door, and I'm in tears on the phone and he says 'What's wrong?' and I tell him they can't find Andres.

So my husband says, hang up on the principal, there's no use staying on the phone, we should call the police and tell the police he's missing. And then my husband got in the car and started driving around, backtracking to the school, looking around the neighborhood for him."

"And I'm thinking, God, this kid barely knows his phone number, and he's got bad hearing in one ear, so if somebody's talking to him, if they're not talking to him in the right ear...." Pilar pauses. "You think the worst things at a time like that. You don't know what to think, and you think everything at the same time."

"So I call the police, and they come, and I give them a description, exactly what he was wearing that day, and they were looking all over for him, and so is my husband. So then I heard the bottom door opening and closing, and I figured it was either my husband or it was Leigha, or maybe my mother, because I'd called her, too. And I ran to the door, and there's Leigha, my daughter," says Pilar. "She's coming in with Andres, and I looked and I couldn't talk, I couldn't even breathe. I just grabbed him, and then Leigha says, 'Mom, Andres was on my bus.' And I said, 'What?'"

"Out of the million buses that go through this city, somehow the teacher puts him on the wrong bus, and when the bus driver figures out he's got an extra boy on his bus, he says, 'Don't worry, I'm going to get you home as soon as I drop off all these other big kids, from the middle school. I'm going to take you right to your house.'"

"And then by some miracle, Leigha, who's at Lincoln, says she's the first person onto the bus, and who does she see sitting there but Andres, and she said, 'What are you doing on the bus?' And the bus driver said, 'You know him?' And she said, 'That's my little brother.'"

Pilar pauses. "So the next day, I can't let him go. I wouldn't let him go to school, I was so afraid to get him back on that bus. Now I think if he senses that I'm afraid, he's going to be afraid. I should send him. But I couldn't do it. So the day after that, I followed the bus to school. I followed the bus to school and when he got out of school I was there, fifteen minutes early. I watched the teacher. I made sure she put him on the right bus, and I followed the bus home. I just did it that one day. I needed to give myself peace of mind that this was going to be done right."

"I think of that when I'm talking to parents up against the [school] system," says Pilar. "And I remember how scared I was, and how furious I was over some of the stuff that happened."

"It's important to remember how important every child is to their parent."

• • •

GIVEN HER PERSONAL AND PROFESSIONAL commitment to school choice, I ask Pilar what led her to leave her job as parent organizer. "I just decided I had to stop for awhile. I was living school choice. Dreaming about it," she says. "I was at so many parent meetings, and on the phone even at home that I was hardly seeing my own kids. They were telephone orphans. I mean, I left work, came home, and the phone would ring. The parents that needed to talk to me couldn't call until their workday was over," Pilar recalls. "And all this time I didn't have a wireless phone, so I was really tied to the telephone, stuck in this little corner of my house."

Pilar's hiatus didn't last long. A few months after the injunction that halted the expansion of Milwaukee's choice program, Pilar had an idea that energized all of her activist impulses. She decided to run for political office, challenging the sitting state representative in her 8th Assembly district.

"I live in a predominately Hispanic district," says Gomez. "But knowing that a lot of Hispanics typically don't vote, I knew I couldn't count on that. I had to run on my principles, and run on what I believe, how I could affect the community or work with people to help them do things for themselves."

Pilar had gone to high school with Walter Kunicki, the well-known state representative she had decided to run against. "We go way back. I mean, my brother-in-law is his best friend, and he's even been his campaign manager. I told him, in terms of dirt, let's not go there and do that. Let's just run a very positive type campaign, and let's talk about the issues that affect people. He was agreeable to that and that's what we stuck with."

Primary day came, and brought Pilar's candidacy to a halt. "I finished fourth out of five," she says. "Hey, I beat the only Republican."

"The way I look at it, you either want to win or you need to win. I wanted to win," says Gomez, "but I didn't need to."

"The whole reason I ran was to give [Kunicki] a wake-up call," Pilar continues. "I needed him to get back into knowing what the community wanted. I think it made a difference in the fact that he had to go out and knock on doors, that he had to re-connect with people. I think he realized how disconnected he was, how he had a very powerful position being the minority leader and former majority leader [in Madison], but he didn't use that power to effectively impact our community like he probably could have."

"I knew I was running against a good guy, but I did it anyway. My point was well taken," says Gomez, who is on good terms with Kunicki, in spite of his opposition to allowing religious schools to participate in Milwaukee's choice program. "To this day he still tells me 'thank you.'"

"It was a very positive period, because I used a lot of the knowledge that I gained from being a targeted investment neighborhood coordinator and with Parents for School Choice and tried to put it to work."

I ask Pilar whether she would ever run for office again.

She smiles. "I still have all my extra lawn posters in my basement. I mean, I don't know when it will happen again, but I think it's inevitable for me. I'm just the kind of person who likes to get involved."

Carol Butts with her kindergarten class at Clara Mohammed School.

CAROL BUTTS

*"...You have to nurture the whole
child, academically, socially, emotionally.
Everything that this child needs, you
have to be the provider."*

"I had been aware of Clara Mohammed for a while, maybe a couple of years," Carol Butts recalls of her visit in the late summer of 1998 to the private school on Milwaukee's Near North Side. "But I was never in a position to go there, given the tuition. I really couldn't afford it, but it was always in the back of mind: Wishful thinking, you know. And really, I was happy with the way things were at King," Dr. Martin Luther King, Jr. School, an elementary MPS specialty school, offering an Afrocentric immersion program. Yet when Butts's two oldest boys left King for middle school at MPS's Malcolm X Academy, what had been a positive public school experience quickly soured.

"Malcolm X was where most of the kids from King went," explains Butts. "It was [Afrocentric] immersion, too, so I thought it would be pretty much a continuation" of the experience her children had had at King. "But it was really different," Carol says. "I wasn't pleased at all."

"At King they were really organized, they had good principles, good morals and values, and I thought this carried on to the middle school," said Carol. "But I found out it didn't." Butts noticed that some of Malcolm X's most committed parents were leaving the school. She and her husband LeRoi began to wonder whether the time had come to pull their kids, too. But before Carol did that, she had to see what her educational options were.

"So I went over to [Clara Mohammed School] to meet with the principal, to see what we could work out in terms of tuition and such, to make it possible for my kids. My thinking was, okay, if I got a second job, maybe there's a way. Sister Basimah [Basimah Abdullah, Clara Mohammed's principal] and I, we hit it off. I mean, we just clicked from the very beginning. She told me about the choice program, which was coming on for religious schools at the time. She said, 'So cross your fingers, because if it does come in, it will be a blessing for the school and for you as well.'"

At one point in the conversation, Basimah Abdullah asked Carol what she did. "Carol told me she was teaching at a childcare center," says Abdullah, "but that she really wanted to open her own pre-school. As a principal, when I hear something like that, that's a flag for me. Not everyone loves to be around babies that much." Abdullah had an opening for a kindergarten teacher; she asked Butts whether she'd be interested.

"Basimah said, 'You need to work for me!' I took her to be joking, really," Carol recalls. "I told her: I didn't come looking for a job, you know. I came to find somewhere for my children to go to school. But Basimah said, 'Well, you think about it.'"

"And I said, 'I might just take you up on that.'"

Carol Butts's connection to the Clara Mohammed community had begun.

• • •

CLARA MOHAMMED IS A HARD SCHOOL TO FIND. Armed with the address, I drive up and down Wright Avenue, through the intersection of Martin Luther King, Jr. Avenue several times, to no avail. Finally, I park in the lot of a Kentucky Fried Chicken, call the school on my cell phone, pen in hand, ready to write down directions again. A woman answers. "You see the KFC?" she asks me; I tell her I'm in the parking lot. "Okay, face it. Now turn directly around and look at the building across the street, right on the corner. That's us." I comply, and find myself looking at the same storefront advertising formal-wear rental that I've passed at least three times. Then I see it: A hand-lettered sign hung in the window.

"A school is a building with four walls
and tomorrow's future inside."

Inside the school, Basimah Abdullah walks me up a back staircase, floor-boards creaking as we go. In the classrooms, the children seem happy, boys in their white shirts and blue pants, girls with navy or white veils covering their hair, and the teachers are all business. Yet, I can't help but be surprised at the well-worn paint on the walls that advertise the hard use the building has seen. I chalk it up to a school that clearly must have just moved into the old, unrefurbished commercial site. As Basimah tours me through the school, I casually ask how long it's been since Clara Mohammed moved into the building. "Oh, forever," she says. "The school's been here for 27 years."

• • •

WE SIT CROSS-LEGGED AND SHOELESS in Clara Mohammed's carpeted prayer room on the school's second floor. The baseboard heaters are turned off, and it's not long before the cold Milwaukee winter seems to seep up through the floorboards. Carol Butts is talking about the concerns that brought her to Clara Mohammed.

"I wanted teachers who could be role models for my children, I wanted moral values and ethics, and I found that here. In looking at the curriculum and their program I said, okay, this is what they need."

"As I say, I didn't know about the choice program at the time. But I was driven, regardless, so it really didn't make much of a difference. But then, in August we got the call, and they said, you need to come in and do your actual paperwork. Choice had been approved and it was no problem. It was very comfortable, to know that I could get all of my children in."

It had been six years since Carol Butts and her husband had moved to Milwaukee from Chicago; for her oldest son, Timothy, Clara Mohammed would be his fifth new school.

"As a kindergartener, Timothy was assigned to Palmer Elementary School in the MPS system. He was bused at that time. Timothy stayed at Palmer for two years and then we moved. Then he went to 95th Street school, way out," Carol recalls, "bused again. He failed second grade." Two years later, the Butts family moved again; Timothy and his brother Brandon were enrolled in MPS's Dr. Martin Luther King, Jr. School. Even with a sibling preference policy, MLK didn't have room for Carol's youngest children. "People didn't leave. So if your child went there in kindergarten, you kind of stayed, and you were lucky." With transfer space scarce, Carol's daughter, Evan, and her youngest son, Quentin, attended 21st Street School.

At the time, private school was not on Carol Butts's priority list. "I was really happy with King. I liked the immersion program. I wanted to continue with it because it was really working for my boys."

When the time came to leave King for middle school, Butts, like many other King parents, chose Malcolm X Academy. Already an involved parent, Carol Butts quickly made herself a presence at Malcolm X. "At this age, my boys are reaching puberty, and they're very impressionable. So to know what was going on at their school, I worked over there. I sat on the Village Council at Malcolm X and I was trying to help the school make some changes. I worked as the Parent Center person there with Greater Milwaukee Education Trust."

"I had some concerns, and I was willing to be a parent who would work to make things better," recalls Butts. "But then the changes started."

During the summer of that year, Malcolm X changed principals. "Didn't tell the parents anything," recalls Carol. "We came back to school for the new year, and here was a new principal assigned, and this really made it worse. He was not for anything that we were for."

"We never got an explanation of why the old principal left. We had no knowledge that he was leaving, that he was considering leaving or had given his notice. And at that time, at the beginning of the new school year, nobody had any answers for us. It was done totally under the table. They hadn't talked to parents at all. We were really displeased with that," Carol explains. "And then the structures, activities, and things that we had started trying to implement, all of that was just washed out now, because you've got to get used to a whole new administration."

Parents began to fear that the departure of Malcolm X's old principal signaled a shift in the school's philosophy. "The mission statement of the school, you know, was to get your children through the 'rites of passage,'" says Carol, "and to do that, it takes a series of steps and procedures." As Butts saw it, the casual way in which MPS shuffled principals "just defeated the purpose of the program, and the progress we'd made went right out the window."

"A lot of the teachers had been moved and transferred, had left, they'd gotten so frustrated. Every teacher that I think had a vast interest in what our children were doing had either been moved or transferred," says Butts. "So as a parent, I got the impression that they [MPS] wanted the program to fail."

"Now Evan's in the fifth grade and she's getting ready to go to middle school. Evan is our only girl, and I'm looking at Malcolm X and saying: 'What's going on here?' Everything was mass confusion. It was terrible."

Butts and her husband faced a difficult decision. "Well, as I say, with two of my sons there I still was very leery about my daughter coming in. I didn't want to bring her into the turmoil, plus, for my daughter, I was looking for some positive female role models within the school that she could connect with. At that point I was thinking, okay, well maybe I can mother the boys through, because with the rites of passage and all of the programs that they have for black males, maybe I can work with [Malcolm X] and get them through it."

Where to enroll Evan remained a problem. Butts applied to MPS's public school selection program, but did not get any of her three choices. "They were saying because of the neighborhood that we lived in, she was going to have to go to Malcolm X, because that was the neighborhood school. And I was saying, no, I'm not going to bring her into this program so I've got to do something here. As I say, at that time, I didn't know anything about [the] choice [program] at all, so I was thinking if I've got to change jobs, take on a second job, that's it then," says Butts. "Because if MPS is not going to invest in this program, then to me, I'm already defeated."

• • •

FOR CAROL BUTTS, CLARA MOHAMMED proved precisely the kind of school she wanted for Evan. "It being a religious school, just for morals and the values that they teach, was so phenomenal, because it was just what I was looking for for my daughter."

"Women have such a hard time in society as a whole. With what we see on T.V., in movies, and in society, women and especially teenagers, our girls, they're not seeing strong, positive role models." At Clara Mohammed, Butts liked the level of respect toward women and girls, as well as the role female teachers and the school's principal, Basimah Abdullah, played in the school.

Carol enrolled Evan for sixth grade and her youngest son, Quentin, for fifth grade at Clara Mohammed, but she didn't move her older boys immediately. "I didn't want to force it on them, so I just kind of let it be a model."

"Brandon had been with my mom in Chicago for the summer, and he had kind of decided he was going to stay up there with Grandma and go to school," recalls Butts. "So that was okay. And then Timothy was still at Malcolm X, and I said, 'Well okay, well maybe I can get Timothy through.'"

The school year started at Clara Mohammed about three weeks before it did in Chicago, and Carol spent several phone conversations telling Brandon about Evan's and Quentin's new school. "So at one point, he said, 'Well okay, maybe I'll come back and try school there." Brandon returned, leaving Timothy at Malcolm X. The split created some tension between the Butts children. "I mean, we're struggling because [Clara Mohammed] is a small school," explains Carol Butts. "There's not many activities, and here Timothy is in seventh grade, with lots of things to do at Malcolm X. He's not really ready to give all that up, so I'm not forcing him to change."

"So first semester, he's there, but they've changed so many teachers that he's not focused now. And the year before, because I was there and I was vocal, I made sure that he had good teachers, but now, the administration changed. Things are different," says Butts. "But I said, okay, we're going to give it some time." By November, Timothy's grades had dropped drastically. "He wasn't focused, and I wasn't getting feedback from the school," Butts recalls.

Timothy joined his brothers and sister at Clara Mohammed just before Thanksgiving. Though he had been struggling at Malcolm X, Timothy Butts tested at the eighth grade level on achievement tests administered at his new school; Basimah Abdullah told Timothy to report to eighth grade at Clara Mohammed.

• • •

CLARA MOHAMMED ENROLLS 105 children from age three through ninth grade. Eighty-five of the 105 attend on choice vouchers. With just seven ninth graders and eight eighth graders, Timothy and Brandon shared a classroom. "There's no such thing as, 'You don't do your homework,'" says Carol Butts. "You can't hide behind the kid in front of you."

"I'm really very pleased," says Carol Butts, speaking about the progress of her own children. "The 15-to-20-student/teacher ratio is excellent. [My children's] grades have improved, and their outlook, too," Butts notes. "They really can see the madness in other schools now. You'd never know it, I guess—you'd think that was the only way things could be, until you've seen some contrast to it."

I ask Butts if she thinks Clara Mohammed could survive without the choice program. "Choice is a big part of our enrollment now, yes. But they maintained this school for 25 of the past 27 years one way or another, without the program. And if the school has maintained without it for 25 years, in this community that means that the morals and values here are grounded and people believe in this school," says Carol.

"We're trying to look for a new building, because last year enrollment jumped from 64 to 105. The word's out. If you look around, our school is not the most attractive school. We don't have a lot of things, so [the increase in enrollment] says something about what we're doing inside," says Carol Butts.

"We're up against so many other MPS schools with basketball teams and football teams, and all kinds of activities. So, what makes students want to stay here? Because here they're not a number, they're not another student in a student body of 700."

"They know your children here," Carol continues. "If they're having a bad day, the teacher knows it, the principal knows it. Kids really need that."

• • •

I ASK CAROL WHY SHE CHOSE TEACHING. "When we moved to Milwaukee, Timothy was in kindergarten, and I enrolled my younger children in SDC [Milwaukee's Social Development Commission] Head Start. And that's where I really got a love for [teaching]."

With each child a year behind the other, Carol's Head Start experience lasted four years. "It got me used to being involved in my children's education, and that's where I got my love for just being with students. I worked with Head Start on their policy making council for a number of years. I was the chairperson for the City of Milwaukee with Head Start. It started out as volunteer [work]. Then I actually went to work for the commission, but not in Head Start. Just to get off the ground, I worked with the Energy Assistance Program as a liaison. And then I decided to go to school, to take the classes you need to certify to teach Head Start, to work with three- to five-year-olds.

"I worked with them for a few years and then I was a Kindercare lead teacher. I was the Kindercare manager. So when Sister Basimah asked me [to teach at Clara Mohammed]," Butts recalls, "it just seemed right."

When I note that it's hard to distinguish between Carol's comments as a teacher and a mother, she tells me: "Because I don't. You know, a kindergarten or a preschool teacher is really a mom to that child, because in most of today's society, that teacher is actually with the child more hours of the weekday than the mom is. The mom gets the child up and out in the morning, drops him off to school, and she's off to work."

"Most parents are done with work at 6:00. So children leave here at 3:30; if there's an after school program that day, they're here. If not, they go to another child's home or day care or an after school program until 6 o'clock, right? Then that parent picks them up, feeds them dinner, then it's a bath and to bed. So those kids have been with the parent maybe two hours that day," says Carol, "and their teacher six to seven hours."

"That's why you have to nurture the whole child, academically, socially, emotionally: everything that this child needs, you have to be the provider for that during that time. I think it's sad that public schools and the school system, period, haven't connected with home and community. It's sad that they haven't because a lot of our children get lost in the cracks because of this. I don't fault the teacher per se," says Butts. "I fault the system. You know, could I lock you in a room with 35 five-year-olds and tell you: 'Function?' There's no way that one person can attend to all the social, developmental, emotional needs of 35 different other individuals. I have ten [students], and it's all I can do."

As Carol Butts sees it, schools like Clara Mohammed are up against an uncaring system. "Most of our parents are single moms or grandmoms or people who are trying hard to keep a connection between school and home. But with the way the system has changed these last three to five years with welfare reform and with 'school to work,' it has been a traumatic impact on our children as a whole. Most parents who are 'at home' moms were forced to go back to work, maybe even take two jobs, to actually be able to support a family. And it has destroyed the sense of family in the community, so the only place that a child gets the structure of a family is at school."

"I think we understand the needs of the family," says Carol. "Our principal comes in here at 7:15 for children who need to be here early because their mom or dad has to go to work. Even now, we're done at four," says Butts, "but you come here, we're here to 5:30 sometimes because some mommy has to work till five o'clock, because we don't have bus transportation, so you're here with that child who has to stay 'til mom can pick him up."

"And we don't have an after-school program. There's no extra cost or extra fees we get out of it."

"The students here care. They care about one another," says Carol. "That connection makes up for all the extra-curricular activity they don't have. They want to go skating together, they want to go shopping together, they want to do these things together on the weekends. Whereas you don't get a lot of that, especially when you've been bused all over the city, you don't really get a chance to interact with friends as a family. You can't keep that school connection in the rest of your life."

I ask Carol, if the school had a credo or a mission statement, what would it be? "If you didn't see the sign on the door [of the prayer room]," she instructs me, "look at it when you go out. It says, 'None of you believes until he wishes for his Brother what he wishes for himself.' We try to teach that on a daily basis."

"I have a rule in my classroom," explains Carol, "where if somebody does something wrong to somebody, they have to really be accountable for their actions—because I'm trying to deter violence at a very young age. So if a child hits another or bumps someone, and they say 'sorry, sorry,' you know, usually whenever they say that they never mean it."

"I tell my class, nobody in my class says they're sorry. There are no sorry people here. That's not acceptable. You say, 'I apologize for hitting you and I will not hit you again.' Because it makes them own or connect with the responsibility for their actions. It gives them a binding contract, that if I do it again, there are consequences and the next time it happens, you knew what you were doing. You acknowledged it, so now you have a consequence which probably would be the time-out chair. It's just too easy to say 'sorry, sorry' and forget about it."

Carol continues, "If [the confrontation is] physical, there's one more thing. After the apology, the child has to hug the other one. And when you've been fussing and fighting, they don't always want to do that."

"So I say, well, if you are really mad at this person, you're still going to hug them, and now you have an even better reason to do whatever you do to get along with them," says Sister Carol, laughing, "because you don't want to hug them anymore."

• • •

CLARA MOHAMMED IS A MUSLIM SCHOOL, with influence of its faith-based mission evident everywhere, from the chadors worn by its female teachers, to the posters with sayings from the Koran in both English and Arabic script hanging in the hallways. The largest of the warren of rooms that comprise the school is the prayer room in which we sit.

Of the school's 105 students, 40 are Muslim, while 65 are not. Yet all of the students, beginning in kindergarten, spend a part of the day studying Arabic, the language of the Koran. The Arabic teacher, an émigré from Jordan, is Hafeez: the designation in Islam for a person who has committed the Koran to memory, front to back.

Clara Mohammed is in session for two of the five daily prayers Muslims offer to Allah. "Our first prayer comes after the sun reaches its zenith," explains Basimah Abdullah, "about one o'clock. All the children come up [to the prayer room] for that one. We used to do the call to prayer over the PA, but right now, the PA's broken," says Sister Basimah, "so the boys make the call to prayer in the hall outside the prayer room. We switch off. It's quite a competition to see who gets to recite the call."

"At 2:15, only our Muslim children come for the next prayer." I ask why. "It gets too disruptive. To pray you must have clean hands," Sister Basimah tells me. "So that means we've got the little ones splashing water in the sink. The prayer only takes about three minutes. Getting everyone up to the room and back again is a real production."

I observe to Carol Butts that the ACLU and People for the American Way would be quick to spot the subtle coercion in a school culture built so firmly on faith; she disagrees.

"We honor all of the students here. Go and look through our applications, at all of these reasons parents put down on the applications when they say, 'Why do you send your child here?' It's discipline, structure, moral values. Not that we're Muslim," says Butts. "None of our students who are not Muslim are forced to pray."

I ask what non-Muslim children do during prayer. "We pray at the pre-scribed time, and what we say is, if you want to pray in the manner that you pray in," answers Carol, "then that's what you do. They can go over in the corner and pray, or they can just wait until we're done and sit quietly. All we ask is respect."

"We encourage all our children to bring things from their own religion to share with their classmates. We encourage them in that way because, like I say, we're nurturing the whole family here, and when we go to talk about Islamic studies and the Koran, we say, we can tell you why we believe what we believe. Why do you believe what you believe? What's the history behind it? What morals and values do your family bring to the table that you can share with us, because there's one God, and all of his messages are the same: Universal."

"What we basically found is, that most of the children had no connection with the higher being. They had no connection and they needed a sense of belonging. They hadn't found it in their family structure, and they needed a sense of belonging and we let them know that it doesn't have to be [Islam]."

"I teach my children that, yes, I'm a Muslim, and this is what I believe," says Carol. "This is the way that I train you and I rear you up, but at some point in time, you have to find God within yourself, and you have to create a belief system for you. Our two may be the same and they may not be, but even them being the same they're still going to be different because your relationship with God is your own."

"That's the reason, partly, that we have so many problems with our teenagers. They don't have a personal relationship with God. They don't realize that there's a higher being, so they feel like, if I get into trouble, the only person that they might have to answer to, that can do something for me, is the police," Carol continues, "and that's if they catch you."

"And they don't even know that whenever they get into a moment of despair that they can reach down within and find a higher being within their self, because that's where God is: God lives within self. They don't reach down there, to the God that they have, that lives within them. This is why they commit suicide, this is why they commit crimes, this is why they do all the things that they do, because they haven't been grounded in the foundation of love of God and self."

• • •

WE'RE JOINED BY ESSIE,[5] a woman who lives in the Clara Mohammed neighborhood, who for the past three years has been foster mother to six troubled children, ages eight, seven, six, five, four, and three. Essie has three grown children and grandchildren, all of whom live in the area, or in her home. "No matter how the day starts," she jokes, "I always just count on cooking dinner for twelve."

Essie is not Muslim, nor are her six foster children. Yet she enrolled the four school-age children at Clara Mohammed after she became convinced public school was not a good fit for them. Essie saw Clara Mohammed as a positive influence; the children's birth mother, however, did not. And although her children had been stripped from her, her right to a say in their upbringing remained. She convinced the judge overseeing her case that a Muslim school was not right for her children. "So after a year and a couple of months this year," says Essie, "the judge ordered the kids to go to public school."

"I had to explain to [the children] that I did not make this decision. I told them, the judge did, because your mom asked for you to go to a different school. So they understood it."

Essie is fighting to win permanent custody of her foster children. If she does, she'll use the choice program to re-enroll the children at Clara Mohammed.

"The reason I chose for my children to come to Clara Mohammed was that when my children started coming to me, they never had any religious structure, they never knew what it was to go to a church or anything. I go to church, but I mean, I can't go to church every Sunday like a lot of people do. That's wrong," Essie continues, "because I should get up and go. But I knew

---

[5.] Essie is a pseudonym.

that my children could come here, while they were allowed to come here, and learn a constructive religion."

For Essie, the advantages of Clara Mohammed are less instruction in the Muslim faith than the way that faith informs the school's approach to each student. "Here, they got a lot of one-on-one. They were able to come here and have the comfort, the safety and the compassion, the understanding that Sister Carol and the other teachers were able to give them," says Essie. "They were able to give them a very structured and safe place to be."

"You know, they have a long way to come to normal." Essie pauses. "They didn't know what compassion was until they came to me and here to Clara Mohammed. I mean, my kids were the type of children that if you go like this to them," Essie raises her hand from her side unexpectedly. "They're going like this." She flinches, as if expecting to be hit.

Carol Butts had two of Essie's foster children in her kindergarten class. "They were doing a great job here," she says. "I had just started to really get responses from them, even after a year, to get them where they were comfortable, to where they were finally ready to really begin learning, because the first year was about just being able for them to learn to trust me. For them to be able to be given a lot of love but me still being firm. Some days it wasn't even pushing the work; it was just, okay, sit in my lap, suck your finger if you need to, get a hug."

Essie finds teachers take a different attitude toward her foster children at their new public school. "What I'm seeing [at the children's public school] is them always being moved to a different table, the teachers singling them out as trouble makers, putting a label on them as children who have emotional problems," says Essie. "And I think that's very unfair."

"The littlest one," says Essie, "he sucks his fingers constantly. That's just the way he feels his comfort zone, and the teachers at the school he goes to now, they write him up for this. They're not seeing that this child has a severe social connection problem. But instead of them saying, here why don't you draw or write, give him something to think about, they write him up. So when I tried to talk to the teacher about this, her response was 'I'm not a baby sitter, I'm a teacher.' And I said, 'Well, you know, we all have to do a little bit more than what our job description tells us to.'"

Carol Butts concurs. "I mean, if you make the day about chiding him about sucking his fingers, then that's what the day is about. And the child doesn't learn anything."

"That's what makes teaching such a very hard job," Butts continues, "because you have to connect with each child in a group and as an individual, and you cannot force them to function. You have to bring them to this setting gradually, and you actually have to prepare almost a lesson plan for each individual child to connect. For one child, learning one new letter in a whole day may be the milestone that you set for that child. You have to accept that, and understand that each child is an individual and that they all learn at their own pace," says Carol. "You can't force it or fight it, or you get nowhere."

Essie continues: "The teacher [in the public school] says, 'He has to learn the things,' and I told her, he is learning, whether you know it or not, by him doing his drawings and scribbling on his paper, this is him letting something out inside. You have to deal with children on an individual level."

• • •

AS ESSIE LEAVES, I RETURN to the issue of religion and school choice.

"With people against the choice program, the religious issue always comes up," says Carol. "That's what upsets me a lot, when people say the choice program isn't any good. This country is founded on 'In God we trust,' so the country acknowledges that God is first, and that's right. Your connection with God is your connection with every other human being," says Butts. "In Islam, this is love, it's stronger than the universe. It's the only thing that binds living things to other living things. That's the concept our forefathers grounded this country on."

Butts shakes her head. "Why not give these children, these teachers, what they need to nurture and help our children grow, so we don't have the drugs, so we don't have the violence, so we don't have the Columbines?"

"We see a lot of quote–unquote 'leaders' in this community who say they want to re-connect neighborhoods, they want to re-connect communities," says Carol. "But they don't. Here we are with a program that is allowing youth to go to some schools that they live near. Where they don't have to get on the bus, when all that busing does is break the connection to community."

"When they attack choice schools," Butts says, "it makes you wonder if they really want communities to work."

• • •

A KNOCK ON THE PRAYER ROOM DOOR interrupts us. Sister Carol is needed back in her class. In a few minutes, the sun will reach its zenith, and Carol Butts's four children as well as her ten kindergartners will join the other children of Clara Mohammed on the carpet of the prayer room, facing out across Dr. Martin Luther King, Jr. Avenue towards a distant Mecca, to offer the mid-day prayer.

Chapter Two
CLEVELAND

CLEVELAND

FIVE YEARS PASSED between the enactment of Milwaukee's break-through parental choice program and passage of a similar, single-city pilot program in Cleveland in July 1995. The Cleveland Scholarship Program commenced in the 1996–97 school year, and currently enrolls 3,400 students in 53 private schools across the city, approximately 5 percent of all school-age children in Cleveland. In contrast to the Milwaukee program, which initially allowed vouchers to be used only at non-religious private schools, the Cleveland program was from its inception open to the city's religious schools. As a result, in August 1996, more than a thousand low-income Cleveland children became the first ever to use publicly funded vouchers to attend the religious school of their choice. At $2,250 per child, Cleveland's vouchers were about one-third the average per-pupil expenditure for the city's public school students.[6]

As in Milwaukee, the Cleveland program immediately became the target of a tireless legal assault waged by state affiliates of the American Federation of Teachers and National Education Association, joined by their anti-voucher allies in People for the American Way and the American Civil Liberties Union. While the Cleveland program was upheld at the trial court level in August 1996, just two weeks before the beginning of the school year, voucher opponents persevered through the appeals process, mounting First Amend-

[6.] "The Equity Gap," *Cleveland Plain Dealer,* March 25, 1997.

ment church-state objections in addition to challenging the Cleveland program on procedural grounds. In the spring of 1997, an Ohio appeals court struck down the Cleveland voucher program, holding that it violated both the U.S. Constitution's religious establishment clause and an Ohio state constitutional clause requiring all laws to apply equally throughout the state. That summer, the Ohio Supreme Court agreed to hear the case, and granted a stay pending its ruling. As voucher students reported to school for the 1997–98 year, the Cleveland Scholarship Program was in legal limbo.

In May 1999, less than one month before the completion of the CSP's third school year, the Ohio Supreme Court ruled the Cleveland voucher plan unconstitutional on procedural grounds—the Cleveland plan had been passed as part of an omnibus budget in 1995, rather than single-subject legislation—while upholding the program on the substantive church-state issue. As the school year drew to a close, it seemed the Cleveland Scholarship Program was dead.

Within the month, however, the Ohio legislature re-enacted the Cleveland program. Predictably, the teachers unions and People for the American Way immediately sued to stop the program, this time in federal court. In late August 1999, on the eve of the new school year, federal judge Solomon Oliver first granted and then partially reversed an injunction against the Cleveland program pending his ruling, allowing students already receiving choice vouchers a one-semester reprieve. In December 1999, five days before Christmas, Judge Oliver struck down the Cleveland program. Sandra Feldman, president of the American Federation of Teachers, hailed the ruling as evidence that "the voucher sideshow" would now take its place as "a fad of the past."[7]

Counsel for CSP parents and students are appealing Judge Oliver's ruling, setting in motion the fifth court case in the program's four-year history. Both parties to the suit have agreed not to seek an injunction in the case. As a result, the 3,400 children enrolled in the Cleveland voucher program have a "stay of execution" as the appeals process moves forward.

---

[7] AFT press release, December 20, 1999.

Cleveland Scholarship & Tutoring Program

Eligibility:
- Priority given to students from families with income below 200% of the federal poverty level
- Grades K–6 eligible in1999–2000; program expands one grade per year
- Resident of the Cleveland Municipal School system
- Students selected by lottery, if more applicants han scholarships available

Value of voucher:
- Maximum of $2,250 for 1999–2000 year
- Parents responsible for 10% of tuition

Current participation:
- 3,688 students at 50 schools for the 2000–2001 year
- Program offers 1,000 new scholarships per year

Johnietta McGrady at the McGrady home with her daughter, Trinnietta (top step, right), her son, Atlas (bottom step, right), and grandsons, Reginald (bottom step, left) and Delontae (bottom step, middle).

JOHNIETTA McGRADY

"Every day I wake up, I tell the children, today is another day of Thanksgiving."

"HELLO, MRS. McGRADY, how are you?"

"I'm blessed."

It is the third or fourth time we've spoken by telephone, and each time the response to my throw-away formality is the same. Johnietta McGrady wants the world to know she's not merely "well" or "fine," but "blessed." Over the course of several interviews, I come to the realization that Johnietta means her response to be something of a reminder to herself as well, in sharp contrast to the circumstances that surround her.

At age 41, Johnietta McGrady is a single mother living in the Glenville neighborhood on Cleveland's East Side, raising not only her two youngest children, Trinnietta McGrady and Atlas Phillips, ages seven and six, but her eldest daughter's two sons as well. Eight-year-old Reginald and five-year-old Delontae have been in Johnietta's care for almost four years, since a county court named McGrady legal guardian of her grandsons.

Trinnietta and Atlas attend St. Thomas Aquinas School on 91st and Superior Avenue, two dozen blocks from the McGrady home, with their tuition paid through the Cleveland Scholarship Program (CSP), a voucher program for low-income Cleveland families funded by the state of Ohio. Trinnietta, who finished second grade in June, has never gone to school anywhere else, having received a voucher through the CSP lottery in the spring of 1997. Although Johnietta McGrady had received a second scholarship for her son in the spring of 1999, Atlas's enrollment at St. Thomas was in doubt well into the fall semester, as the injunction against the Cleveland voucher program raised a question whether "new" students like Atlas would be covered.

St. Thomas administrators told Johnietta and other voucher parents to send their children to school; as for the payment of tuition, they'd worry about that later. Johnietta agonized about what she would do to pay the $138 per month tuition for Atlas. "Money was tight as it is," recalls Johnietta. "I guess I was counting on the program being there for [Atlas] like it was for [Trinnietta]." McGrady thought briefly about asking her older brother for financial help; she decided against it, reasoning that it wasn't his responsibility. She came to the conclusion she couldn't keep Atlas at St. Thomas if the voucher program was discontinued; he would have to transfer to public school. In early November, by a 5-4 vote, the U.S. Supreme Court stayed the injunction pending the outcome of the federal court appeal. Cleveland kindergartners would be able to receive their vouchers. Johnietta was off the hook.

Both Trinnietta and Atlas are prospering at St. Thomas. "I feel it's right for them," says Johnietta. With Atlas having just finished kindergarten, McGrady bases most of her judgments on St. Thomas on the experience of her daughter.

"Trinnietta doesn't know how lucky she was," says Johnietta. "I give the credit to her teacher, Mrs. Demascio. She got those children to learn, to really want to learn."

"I had 30 children enrolled," recalls Judy Demascio, Trinnietta's first grade teacher. "Almost half were displaying some difficulty learning. Trinnietta was one of them."

Recalls Demascio: "Trinnietta came into my class below average in terms of achievement. But there was one thing that was clear right away: She was highly motivated. In terms of behavior, she tended to talk, but if you asked her to stop, she would. You could see she had some sort of structure at home, and some support from a parent. I always say if there's some help at home, you can get a child to learn."

As for reaching Trinnietta and her other struggling classmates, Demascio had no time to waste. Brainstorming for ways to lift her students' achievement, she hit on the idea of training parents as tutors, creating the kind of school-to-home link that could reinforce her efforts in the classroom. "I put the word out, and asked parents to come after school, until around six o'clock, once a week," Demascio says. Seventeen parents came to the first few sessions. "I drilled them in phonics, how to recognize word families," says Demascio. "The basics. The things they needed to know to help their children learn to read."

Johnietta McGrady was a regular at the parent sessions. "Mrs. McGrady was always there," Demascio recalls. "Her kids came with her, and her grandkids, too." In time, the parents group dwindled down to six or seven diehards. Mrs. McGrady was one of them.

Despite Mrs. Demascio and her parent/tutors' efforts, too many of the children weren't closing the learning gap. "Between winter break and a couple of snowstorms, we'd lost a month," says Demascio. She was forced to backtrack. By spring, she came to a realization: "Half of my kids weren't going to be ready to move up to Grade 2."

Demascio approached St. Thomas' administrators with a radical plan. She would simply keep her classroom running even after the school year ended, adding on another month of instruction. Her superiors were receptive, provided there was sufficient parent interest. Once again, Demascio approached her parents. "School ended, but we kept going. Fourteen kids came," says Demascio. "Pretty much the same group whose parents had come in for the tutoring sessions." Again, Trinnietta McGrady was one of the students.

"The rest of the school was quiet, but there we were. Same time, 8:00 A.M. to 2:30, same classroom," recalls Demascio. Surprisingly, the transition went smoothly. Says Demascio: "By then I guess the kids were used to me and my crazy ways."

Demascio charged a $50 fee for the summer class, not an insignificant sum to many of her parents, whose family incomes hovered around the poverty line. Her plan, which she kept secret from the parents, was to rebate the money at the end of the session to the families whose children attended regularly. "My experience is that if you get something free," explains Demascio, "you don't appreciate it."

The summer session was a great success. All of the students who attended moved on to second grade, including Trinnietta, who, according to Mrs. Demascio, had improved from below average to average in terms of reading ability. When the session ended and Demascio gave back Johnietta McGrady's $50, McGrady balked. "I said she had to keep it," Johnietta recalls. "[Mrs. Demascio] worked hard. She earned it. She did right by our kids." Demascio refused; Johnietta remains convinced she should not have received her money back.

If Johnietta is pleased with the level of instruction and attention her own children are getting at St. Thomas Aquinas, the education of her grandson Reginald is a different matter. Reginald attends Stephen E. Howe Elementary, a short walk from the McGrady home, the same school Johnietta's son Atlas would have attended if his voucher had not come through.

Even though "Aunt" Trinnietta—Tee Tee, as her mother calls her—is two years Reginald's junior and a grade behind him in school, she regularly spends a part of the homework hour at the McGrady dining room table helping her nephew with his lessons.

"I'm worried about him," Johnietta says of Reginald. "I don't want to see him fall behind." Because Reginald is her grandson and not a sibling of either Trinnietta or Atlas, Johnietta has not received a CSP voucher for him. "I haven't pushed it," she says, "but I'm starting to wonder if whether I should." Clearly, it's a concern for Johnietta, who returns to the issue of Reginald's schooling regularly.

Still she hesitates. Although Johnietta is legal guardian of Reginald and Delontae, even as the children mark their fourth year under her roof, she wars with herself over decisions that imply she is the permanent caretaker of her grandchildren, as if their mother will never be in a position to reclaim her children for her own.

• • •

JOHNIETTA HERSELF IS A PRODUCT of Cleveland's public schools. "I went to Harry Davis Junior High, when my mother brought us up here" to

Cleveland from Demopolis, Alabama, the little town where Johnietta had been born. It was 1970; Johnietta was twelve. Her parents were separated. "My father was always a good provider. Me and my brothers and sisters always had a good relationship with both my parents, going down to Demopolis for summers and so on."

Johnietta's mother came to Cleveland because her cousin, who'd come north from Demopolis years earlier, found her a job. The Monday after she arrived in Cleveland, Beatrice Phillips started work as a dietician at Huron Road Hospital, where she worked for almost 20 years.

In a few years, Johnietta went on to John Hay High School in the Cleveland public system; she got pregnant in tenth grade and dropped out. Johnietta was sixteen when her oldest daughter was born, and on her own.

"I got a job at the TRW factory, over at 185th and St. Clair. It was a good job—valve feeder," Johnietta recalls. "But I felt like a nobody. I got laid off at one time. It gave me time to think. About that time, I was preaching to my daughter, you know, she was heading for junior high then, about how hard going it is out there. How you need school and an education to get by. And I caught myself giving values I didn't apply to myself."

"I was telling my daughter to go to school and be somebody, make something of herself," Johnietta recalls. "Kids at that particular age are very sensitive to that. They say, 'But you didn't do it. Mommy, you didn't finish school.'"

"I just knew my life wasn't going any place," says Johnietta, who remembered a promise she'd made herself. "I always said my goal was to achieve a high school diploma before my parents were deceased. I decided it was time to see if I could."

Johnietta went to Tri-C Community College in downtown Cleveland, and got some information about its GED study program. She enrolled in the study class; by spring 1986, she felt she was ready. Johnietta took the GED exam at Max Hayes Technical High School not far from her home. She was 28, ten years behind her graduating class at John Hay. When the letter came saying she'd passed, she threw a "graduation party" for herself, a get-together with friends and family at her house.

"Only thing I don't have is a class ring," Johnietta says, smiling at the thought of it. "I'd pick the color stone myself, maybe my birth month color or something, because I didn't graduate from John Hay and I didn't really go to Max Hayes, so I'd make it up, you know, 'graduate of the Class of '86.'"

I ask whether she'd seriously thought about getting herself a ring; Johnietta brushes my question away.

"There's plenty of other things to be got before I do something like that."

• • •

IN THE FALL OF 1989, Johnietta's oldest daughter started to attend Shaw High School in East Cleveland. Then Johnietta moved the family to Primrose Avenue, out of the East Cleveland district, and her daughter was bused to Cleveland's West Side, to Lincoln West High School. She attended class sporadically. One day during tenth grade, McGrady's daughter came home and told her mother she was pregnant. She dropped out. "Same age as me," says Johnietta.

"Because she didn't finish school, she felt just like a nobody. 'Cause the jobs that she felt that she could do, you got to have that high school diploma," explains Johnietta. "She didn't."

"So what happened was, she got caught up in 'the life,' doing the wrong sort of things," says Johnietta, "with the wrong sort of people. She would be out with her friends for long periods of time, home late or not at all. With everything that was going on, they," Johnietta's daughter's children, her firstborn, Reginald, and later the baby, Delontae, "weren't getting much attention." Johnietta's daughter had always made ample use of her mother's willingness to keep an eye on her children; she began to drop them off at Primrose more often, for longer periods of time.

"This situation with the children was, I thought, a temporary situation," Johnietta recalls. One weekend, McGrady had kept the boys. On Sunday, she took them over to her daughter's house. She wasn't home, but her friends were there. "She had said to leave them with the people who were there, people that I knew distributed drugs," says Johnietta. With misgivings, McGrady did leave Reginald and Delontae, though she called repeatedly to talk to her daughter. Her daughter's friends always answered. Johnietta's daughter wasn't there.

"They kept telling me my daughter was down to a movie. And you know, I would never hear from her, I never had a telephone call from her. They didn't want me to know what was going on, because they wanted to cover up for her as long as they could," McGrady explains.

Finally, Johnietta drove over to her daughter's apartment. "What I did was, I looked through the cabinets and refrigerator." There was no food, no cereal for Reginald or macaroni and cheese or anything else that he liked, no baby food for Delontae. "So I called 696-KIDS," the help line for situations of suspected child neglect.

"That's when the child welfare people followed it up. They went in there," to Johnietta's daughter's home, "and investigated. They placed the kids in temporary [custody], and when we went to court they gave them to me."

Even so, just where the boys would be permanently placed was an open question. "Neither father wanted either one of them, and that was pretty overwhelming," recalls Johnietta. In fact, as McGrady saw it, neither Reginald's father nor Delontae's were really ready for child-rearing responsibilities.

Johnietta's mother began to talk about taking in her great-grandsons. "There my mom was, talking about it. I knew she was going to try to take the responsibility of taking care of these children, to be a good mother to them as she had been to us."

"That was what my mom had wanted: To take the children," says Johnietta. But Beatrice Phillips was terminally ill. "It was just going to be too much," Johnietta remembers. A foster home for the boys seemed the most likely prospect.

"The thing was that they didn't know if they could keep the boys together, get them into the same foster home. They said, it's just so hard to find someone who will take two, you know. I didn't know when I would see them."

"That's when I decided that, you know, I can do this."

• • •

IN THE END, JOHNIETTA'S DAUGHTER wrote a letter to the court, asking that her mother be allowed to raise the children in her home. The court agreed; the woman they called Grandma Johnny became Reginald and Delontae's legal guardian.

Not long after McGrady took her grandsons in, both of their fathers were jailed. "And then after I had had them for a year, their life kind of seems like it was on track."

"The main thing is, those boys needed to know that they're loved," says Johnietta of her grandsons. "No one was going to tell me that I couldn't provide that."

Johnietta wanted to keep the children together in preparation for the day their mother could take them back. "Because I'm thinking all the time that she'll want to come home," says McGrady of her oldest daughter, "and try to work on getting herself together."

The child welfare people have told Johnietta's daughter that she still has a chance to get her sons back. Says McGrady, "They believe in trying to keep the children with their legal mother, regardless of how bad the situation has been. And, you know, I'm all for that. If my daughter wants to have her children again, I am willing to give her a chance. I haven't given up on the fact that she can change, because you know, I'm a recovering alcoholic. And I changed my life over six years ago. So, it's almost the same road she's on."

"Who's to say that she won't change? You know, if I had everyone giving up on me, where would I be today? But when God got me sober I didn't realize at that point he had a job for me," Johnietta recalls. "To take care of a sick mother and [to] take care of these children, and their education and all those things that seem so hard."

"You know what?" McGrady asks. "They been here with each other four years. My children were relatively small, so it's like they are our family now. And so those things that used to seem so difficult, they're past now."

"Today I know that God helped pull me through the rough part of it."

• • •

THE MCGRADY HOUSE RUNS ON A CLOCK, a timer, to be precise, that sits on the dining room table. "When I get home," says Johnietta, "it's almost 4:30. By the time I sit down and get the homework going and get everything situated, it's time to make dinner. If I have an AA meeting, at the center up the street, most of them start at no later than 7. Sometimes my sister comes over; sometimes I take the kids. If I go there, I'm there till 8:30."

"But all in all, the kids have some stability. On nights when I don't go to a meeting, we go to bed at least by quarter to 8, every night."

The dining room table is where the homework gets done, with Johnietta overseeing Trinnietta and Reginald as Atlas and Delontae play under and around the table.

"The kids had so much homework last year, I had to go buy a timer, because I'm tired myself, and we'd be at the table until 7 at night. The teacher told me, Ms. McGrady, you shouldn't be at the table that long."

"Still, it's my way to keep up on what's going on for them at school. I can see the work they do, and how they do it."

To Johnietta, an orderly atmosphere in the home is crucial. "I try to emphasize to the children that this is of great importance," she says. "To have a fresh mind, to start your day off with magic words like, 'thank you' and 'please.' Orderly words, respectful," McGrady continues. "Not this rap trash all over the radio."

"I don't let them listen to rap music at home. To me, that's cuss words," says Johnietta. "And you can't live in this house with cuss words."

Johnietta's list of cuss words includes more than the usual four-letter entries. "The word 'never,' in this house, that's a cuss word. I don't ever want to hear 'never.' I want them to replace that word with 'whatever:' I can do whatever, you know, whatever I put my mind to."

"Every day I wake up, I tell the children, today is another day of Thanksgiving. And every night, I look back with them over the day and just try to be thankful for the good things in it."

JOHNIETTA MCGRADY'S WOOD FRAME HOME stands last on the block, though not on the corner lot; on that site, separated from the McGrady house by a chain link fence, a pile of rubble sits where a house once was. Johnietta's home is owned by her older brother, Dave, who lives in Istanbul, Turkey, where he teaches school and coaches basketball. Johnietta is proud of the home she's made, but wary of her neighborhood.

"The children really don't have friends in the neighborhood. I mean, I'm real particular about the company that they keep." Says Johnietta: "We've got a full schedule. I keep it that way."

For good reason. Of the city's 224 census tracts monitored by the Cleveland police department, the McGrady neighborhood ranks fifth in arson and burglary, and in the top 10 percent in drug calls and drug arrests.[8] Like Johnietta, most of her neighbors are African-American—98 percent, according to U.S. Census data—with more than a third having migrated to Cleveland from their birthplace in the American South. Half of the adults in Johnietta's neighborhood lack a high school diploma, while 15 percent have less than a ninth grade education; nearly two-thirds of the children in the McGrady neighborhood are being raised in single-parent homes. With an average per-capita income of $7,800, nearly a third of the families living on and around Primrose Avenue live in poverty, with over 40 percent receiving some form of public assistance. While nearly 40 percent of the families in the McGrady neighborhood own their own home, one in seven houses stands vacant.

"This is where I did most of my drinking and so on," recalls Johnietta. "Right here, in this house, in this neighborhood." Even now on the streets around Primrose Avenue, negative examples abound. Passing a man drinking on the corner, McGrady turns even a sidewalk trip to the grocery store into a morality tale for her children. "I tell them, you know, take a moment. Look at this man on the corner. I'll give him a quarter, I'll give him a dime. He doesn't have food, I'll give him some."

[8.] Cleveland Police Census Tract Crime Data Base, 1998.

"But for my son, this is what I instructed him," says Johnietta: "This is the way you would live if you take the street. You'll be a useless individual to society, you know. You'd just be a leech all your life. You leech off this one and that one, all your life."

"I don't shy away from it. I show them."

• • •

JOHNIETTA USES EVERY MOMENT in the morning to instill the proper tone for the day to follow. It starts at breakfast, and continues on in the car ride to Howe Elementary to drop off Reginald, and on to St. Thomas Aquinas, to deposit Trinnietta and Atlas.

"No radio," says McGrady, of her morning car regimen. "That's my time to tell them about my expectations for them. I want them tuning everything out because I need them to know that, look, I have to go to work when I drop them off. I have a job, and when I leave there I have to go to another job. So there are things like foolish behavior at school that I don't need to play a part in."

"I tell the children: You have a choice. Misbehave, and you will get your television taken away from you, your 30 minutes you like to watch 'Sesame Street' . . ."

". . .Or 'The Simpsons,'" Trinnietta chimes in.

"The teacher told me the other day about my son running in the classroom," Johnietta continues. "Hopping on one leg and so on. That's something you would get all of your privileges taken away for. So I told him, don't get me called to school to see the principal for that. Because I cannot tolerate, I will not tolerate, disrespectful behavior."

A Baptist, Johnietta McGrady has no qualms about enrolling her children in a Catholic school. "I want a place with values, the moral teaching my children need," says Johnietta. "Respect, and no nonsense in the classroom." She's not alone: Of the 299 children presently enrolled at St. Thomas Aquinas, only eight are Catholic.

• • •

JOHNIETTA WORKS TWO PART-TIME JOBS to accommodate the children's school schedule. Four days a week, she works as a part-time nutritionist cooking meals at a Head Start program, a six-hour shift that begins after she drives her children to their schools.

The job is new for McGrady: "Last year, I was working part-time as a floater for the Cleveland Board of Education, wherever they needed a school cook. The money was better than what I make now, but problem was, I never knew where I was going to be day to day. You call in the morning and say, 'where do I go?' and you go."

"I was all over town, having anxiety about needing to get to my children's schools if they called me," Johnietta recalls. "I had Delontae and Atlas not in school then. It didn't work. The jobs I have now are much better."

"My job now is really a great job," McGrady confides. "I have a class that comes at 8:30. I fix their breakfast, then I fix their dinner. And I check attendance." The children are three to five years old; a second group of youngsters follows the first. McGrady prepares their meal, then goes to her second job, as a school crossing guard.

"My post is in my neighborhood. You really work it morning and afternoon, so four mornings a week, I have a couple of friends who fill in for me, so I can work at Head Start," McGrady explains. "I cross the kids in the afternoon, five days a week." Juggling the two jobs isn't easy, or without expense; Johnietta pays $65 a month for after-care so that her children are looked after at school until she's home from work.

When school is closed over the holidays, Johnietta is off the clock, at both Head Start and her crossing guard job. She receives no paid vacation. "I'm taking some in and paying some out," says McGrady about paying for after-care to keep her crossing guard job. "But you know what? I'm 41 years old, and if I don't go back into putting some money into Social Security, what will I have?"

"And then you know, you can get complacent just sitting here, just waiting on an income once a month," Johnietta says, referring to welfare. "That's not me. You see, I need to work because this is how I give [my children] their lives. I have to teach them their values, you know, this is how you have to earn what you need."

The tuition bill at St. Thomas Aquinas for Trinnietta and Atlas would be $2,760.

"Without vouchers?" says McGrady. "There's no way we could do it."

• • •

THIS YEAR, JOHNIETTA'S OLDEST DAUGHTER gave each of her sons some money for Christmas; McGrady repeats that she doesn't ask her daughter for support: "I'd just as soon see she keeps it to put her own house in order, to get herself to where she can take care of her children again."

"That's what's first for me."

Lately, Johnietta's daughter has been visiting her sons about once a month. On one recent visit, she told her mother she's pregnant again. "And she's saying now she doesn't want that one. You know, if I have to, I'm giving that one to God, because through all I've been through, I want the Lord to not send that one to me."

Just what will happen if Johnietta's oldest daughter doesn't reclaim her sons, if she won't care for her new baby, if the court rules against the Cleveland voucher program, if Reginald continues to drift through his schooling, Johnietta McGrady does not know.

"God keep me here for these babies. Like it says in the 121st Psalm: 'I lift up my eyes to the hills; from where shall come my help?' That's what I pray," she says. "That's why I must maintain my sobriety level."

"But what I say is, 'Why complain?' I have eyes to see. Who, better than you? For these children, I am the chosen one."

"Right there is honor," says Johnietta. "Right there."

Roberta Kitchen with her children, Tiara, Toshika, Tatiana and DeAntye, on the front steps of their East Side Cleveland home.

ROBERTA KITCHEN

*"I have invested too much to let [the
public schools] turn my children into
something that has a hole in it."*

MOST NEW MOTHERS HAVE NINE MONTHS to prepare for the challenge of raising a child. For Roberta Kitchen, motherhood came without warning one night, in the sudden realization that the mother of the three children in her care would not be coming back.

Not that it was at all unusual for Roberta to be looking after four-year-old Tiffany, one-year-old DeAntye, or the newborn, Tiara, barely one month old. After all, Roberta was godmother to the children's mother, a young woman raised in the pervasive poverty of Cleveland's East Side. Her goddaughter was living with Roberta, trying to straighten out her life. For Roberta, a single woman with a demanding job in a large Cleveland corporation in a downtown skyrise, having the children around was pleasant enough, even if her goddaughter's chaotic life was a chronic source of concern.

"It was a weekday," Roberta remembers, "and I got home a little late. The children were there," with Roberta's sister and mother, who lived in the downstairs half of Roberta's duplex. "But my goddaughter wasn't. My sister told me she'd been gone for hours. I asked, 'Did she say where she was going?' And my sister said, 'Yes, she said she was going down to the store to get a pack of cigarettes.'"

Roberta put the children to bed. "They were too young for anything to register. And I was the mainstay. It was perfectly normal for me to be putting them to bed." She sat up talking to her mother and sister, waiting for her goddaughter to return. At midnight, Roberta went to bed.

"I had work the next morning, but I couldn't sleep," Roberta recalls. "I was livid. I was running through in my mind just what kind of going over I was going to give her when she got back. My goddaughter didn't have a key of her own, so I just kept waiting to hear a knock on the door." Hours went by; no knock. The house was silent.

Some time in the middle of the night, Roberta had a realization. "I remember thinking," Roberta recalls, "this is it."

"She's not coming back."

• • •

MONTHS PASSED. ROBERTA AND THE CHILDREN settled into a routine, with plenty of assistance from Roberta's mother, sister, and brothers. "During this time, I was working, of course," says Roberta, "and looking after the children, talking back and forth with the Department of Human Resources. The children's mother would get me messages: 'I'm trying to get my life together, I'm fine, but I'm not ready to take the children back.'" All that time, the children never saw their mother. Roberta never knew if she was living on the next block, or in some other city altogether.

"So we just went on day to day, to build our lives."

Roberta had tried to mentor her goddaughter. "You know, she's from your average dysfunctional family, welfare all the way down the line, as far back as you could go. Only one person in her family ever held a job: her grandmother. Most were on welfare, on drugs and the like."

"For a while, she lived with me," explains Roberta of her goddaughter. "She tried to change, talked about it, but she lived what she learned. And I tried, but I couldn't pull her out of that. She'd come and go. She'd get in trouble with the police. I kept the kids. It was just an arrangement. She had nowhere else to go."

"She was living on the street, and living the life that goes with that, when you have no job, no means of income. And at that time she had Tatiana."

Roberta's goddaughter was determined to keep her fourth child, but Roberta could see how difficult that was, and how tempting it would be for her goddaughter to leave Tatiana with Roberta, as she had her brother and sisters. "At that time, I didn't allow her to. She could come and visit us, but she couldn't leave Tatiana with me," says Roberta. "My back was already against the wall. I already had the three children, I couldn't have another situation."

"Tatiana and her mother lived in shelter after shelter. They never had a place to stay. That is what her life was like: Tatiana literally lived on the street." Things went on that way for three years. Then Roberta's goddaughter was pregnant again.

"When she delivered Toshika, the social worker saw my name in the file with the other three children, and they called me and asked me, 'Would you take Tatiana and Toshika,'" Roberta recalls, "'for ninety days?'"

Roberta laughs. "I said, okay. Ninety days. Yeah, right."

Roberta knew that bringing a newborn home and integrating Tatiana into the Kitchen household would be a challenge. "Tatiana had just turned three. She had not been socialized at all. She did not know how to play with other kids. She had language like a sailor. She was a survivor. She knew how to manipulate, how to get what she wanted. We had to start at the very beginning."

Ninety days came and went; the children stayed. Roberta Kitchen was now the mother of five.

• • •

FOR ROBERTA KITCHEN, THE VALUE of education is a given. "My father went to school in Alabama through seventh grade," says Roberta. "My mother, I'm not sure. But in our house, education mattered." One of eight children, Roberta was the first of three Kitchen children to go to college. After graduating from Cleveland's East High, Roberta went on to earn her business degree from Central State University, Ohio's only historically black university, in the southwest corner of the state. Not long out of college, Roberta came home to Cleveland and took a job in the audit department at Eaton Corporation, the Cleveland automotive electronics conglomerate. She bought a home, in the Collinwood neighborhood, the same home she and the children live in today.

Even with the responsibilities of raising children and the financial strains that has caused, over the years Roberta has taken graduate-level courses at Cleveland State University near her office, first in psychology, and more recently in education administration.

"The dream I have," Roberta confides, "is one day to start my own school."

Roberta's education in the schooling of her new children began in the mid-1980s, when the oldest girl, Tiffany, entered school. "You got your assignment and sent your child to school," Roberta recalls. "That's more or less how it went. Tiffany started in kindergarten at East Clark Elementary, then they moved her to Euclid Park, a public school in the Collinwood neighborhood for first and second grade, then she went over to Case Elementary, down on East 40th, for third and fourth grade." In addition to attending three schools in her first five years, Tiffany was now making a 140-block bus ride every day. "To me, that was a lot of movement for a grade school child," says Roberta. "I went down to a [Cleveland Public School] board meeting, and asked them, 'How can kids build continuity when they're moved around so much?' I never got a straight answer." The next year, however, Tiffany was moved back to Euclid Park, where she went to fifth and sixth grades.

In retrospect, Roberta's concerns about busing proved ironic. In spite of the distance, "Case was the better school," says Roberta now. "Euclid Park, even in those days, was gang-infested, drug-infested. Tiffany had had a really great experience in fourth grade at Case. She really connected with her teacher, and she did well. Then she was back at Euclid Park and it was all downhill."

Tiffany came home talking to Roberta about the gangs at her school, talk that Roberta tended to discount as exaggeration. "Tiffany even told me one time that a kid who was in one of the gangs had broken her teacher's arm," Roberta recalls. "I happened to be at the school for a teachers' meeting not long after, and here I saw her teacher with her arm in a sling, saying something about a situation with one of the students."

"It took it out of me. You know, with Tiffany and with the other children, I've always really made an effort to have them primped, primed, and ready, from pre-school," says Roberta. "DeAntye even got accepted directly into first grade."

Tiffany "couldn't read well, not well at all," recalls Roberta. While Tiffany was receiving remedial assistance to improve her reading skills, Roberta was concerned that the stigma surrounding the remedial help was counter-productive. "They bring in Chapter 1," says Roberta. "The kids are pulled out for special instruction, and everybody says, 'The dumb kids are going to special reading now.'"

Yet in spite of her reading difficulties, Tiffany was bringing home B's and C's on her report card. "I went to her teacher and said, 'I don't understand how that is.' And I asked to have her graded to her ability. Tiffany's teacher said, 'Compared to other kids in her class, Tiffany is doing great,'" Roberta recalls. "At home, I began to talk to Tiffany, saying, you may have to repeat sixth grade. We talked about how it was important to learn now, and not get caught short later on down the road."

Then report card day came. "Tiffany ran in, and she was bubbling," Roberta recalls. "She said, 'I didn't fail!' So I looked at the report card, and I knew no way could my daughter have really made those grades. They were all B's and C's again."

Roberta went back to Tiffany's teacher. "I said, 'My daughter is not ready. I want her to go to summer school, and try to make up ground.'" The teacher said she hadn't failed. She didn't have D's, so she wasn't eligible for summer school. "I said, 'You know, I'm working, I come home and do the best I can. She needs the summer school structure.'"

Surrounded by substandard classmates, Tiffany was looking good by comparison. "It was at that point I said I want out. I didn't know how I was going to do it financially, but I told Tiffany, 'I've got to get you out.'"

It was the spring of 1992. DeAntye was in third grade, Tiara in first, Tatiana was getting ready to begin kindergarten in the fall, and Toshika was a toddler. "The situation for Tiffany was critical," says Roberta. "But DeAntye was in third grade then at Oliver Perry," the public elementary school to which he'd been assigned. Recalls Kitchen: "It was his third school in three years, and that really wasn't working out either."

"Now, whenever somebody said private school," recalls Roberta, "I saw dollar signs. So when I started thinking private school, I began looking for a second job. Something second shift, that I could get to after I got done downtown. I was having trouble finding something, but I did do some small jobs through Manpower [the temporary employment agency] at that time, just to put some extra money aside." Roberta was talking to her friends and family about how she could swing tuition payments. "Somebody said to me, go down to Cedar Hill," a Christian academy not far from Kitchen's home. "Talk to them. See if they can work something out."

Roberta did. "I took Tiffany to Cedar Hill, and I said, 'I want her to repeat.' She did," recalls Roberta. "Simple as that." Roberta enrolled all four of her school-aged children there. All told, the tuition cost her nearly $6,000.

"I never did find a regular second job that fit my schedule," says Roberta. "Looking back, I think God was keeping me from finding one. I would have never been home anymore. I paid late some months. It was rough, a tough time."

For Tiffany, however, the experience was positive. "At Cedar Hill, they just refused to let [Tiffany] fail. They gave her lots of hugs and it worked. It was the thing she needed. They pulled her through."

From Cedar Hill Christian, Tiffany graduated to Orange Christian Academy, Cedar Hill's sister school, in a southeast Cleveland suburb. Tiffany faltered, bringing home failing marks in some classes. Reading the warning signals, Roberta made the decision to move Tiffany again, this time to a private school called Raintree. "I didn't know what we were going to do. I was literally driving by one day in the car," recalls Roberta, "and I passed this school, and just pulled in and walked into the office. I had to try something that would work for Tiffany. So the next year, we switched schools again."

For Roberta, Raintree proved that "just because a school is private doesn't mean it's perfect."

"One day, it was in the spring, I made an unscheduled visit. When I got in the school, I could hear shouting and laughter like a gym class or a class party was going on down the hall. I really don't know why, but I just went down to the door where the noise was coming from, and poked my head in. It was a classroom; Tiffany was in there, and the noise was incredible. There was a fellow sitting in the front of the class, I thought he must have been the teacher," Roberta recalls, "doing nothing. Just sitting there with his elbows on the desk."

"I just let out at the class," says Roberta, whose quiet demeanor makes picturing such a scene difficult. "I said, 'Your parents pay for this?' That quieted them down a bit, but not much. So I turned to the fellow at the front of the class, and I said, 'You the teacher?' 'That's what they call me,' he said. The kids all just thought that was hilarious, and started fooling around like before." Kitchen left the classroom. "Tiffany had that one year at Raintree, and that was it." The next year, at a private Christian school called Second New Hope, was no different.

"At that point, Tiffany struggling in school was nothing new. But I was out of money and out of options. If I had put her in another [private] high school, I would have been paying for four in grade school and one in a private high school, with that one tuition alone $4,000 or more." So Tiffany enrolled at Collinwood High School, the public school serving Roberta's neighborhood.

In what had become a pattern, Tiffany's adjustment to Collinwood was rocky. "Tiffany was turning eighteen, and she was a lot more interested in turning eighteen than being in school," says Roberta. "She started slow, but then she got to where she brought her D's up to A's. But then Collinwood didn't want to advance her to twelfth grade because she was short some credits. I could just imagine what Tiffany's reaction to that would have been." Roberta feared her daughter might drop out. "Above all, I wanted her to finish school. So we looked at South High," another one of Cleveland's public high schools. "Then about that time, Tiffany came up with the idea of Max Hayes," a vocational high school about 100 blocks from the Kitchen home.

On May 30, Tiffany graduated from Max Hayes. It was the tenth school she had attended since kindergarten.

• • •

Roberta Kitchen looks back on the education of her oldest child with evident regret. "By Tiffany having six years in the public schools, you know, I lost her. I never was able to cultivate that interest and self-esteem. She was getting those grades, but kids know, they know they can't do the work."

"Of all the children, Tiffany really adores her mother. I think it's left her dealing with a fear of rejection all her life. She's always been a child who needs to fit in," says Roberta, "and who just shuts down when she doesn't. You see it in the struggle she's had in school. She either excels, or she totally doesn't. When she connects with her teachers, she can do well. That's the way it was at Case, and it was like that for a while at Collinwood and for the year she was at New Hope, too. It's not that she can't do the work. That's a big source of my disappointment," says Roberta. "That Tiffany has shown that she *can* achieve."

Her oldest daughter's difficulties strengthened Roberta's desire to keep Tiffany's younger siblings in private school. "I was discouraged by the public school experience with Tiffany. That's a big part of why I am so set on finding the right private school for them, and keep them there."

• • •

If in spite of all her efforts Roberta's children face more challenges than most kids, none face more than Tatiana. Spending her first, formative years on the streets is a disadvantage she is still working to overcome.

"Even at school, if she was picked on, she fought back," says Kitchen. "She had mastered that. She was drawn back to what she learned on the streets." Tatiana could fend for herself. What she couldn't do was trust. "It's nearly ten years now, and we're still working on that, still working on her trust level."

When the time came for Tatiana to start school, she took her socialization problems with her. For kindergarten through second grade, Kitchen had enrolled Tatiana in Cedar Hill, a Christian school in a nearby Cleveland sub-urb—the same school that had provided Roberta's oldest daughter Tiffany with one of her few positive school experiences. With Tatiana, things were difficult. Roberta recalls: "Tatiana's talked all her life. Well, she talked in school. She stood up when she should sit down. That's the way it was." Roberta went to great lengths and to significant financial hardship to avoid having to enroll Tatiana in public school; still, she found it difficult to find a private school that was right for the child.

It was the spring of 1996; one day, Kitchen got a call from a friend who worked at the Cleveland Board of Education. "She said, 'Roberta, did you get the form for this new program to get a private school scholarship for Tatiana and Toshika?' And I had no idea what she was talking about," recalls Roberta. "Now, at that time, my friend knew I was at my wit's end, so she said, 'Never mind, I'm going to fill it out for you. Just sign it and fax it back.'"

The Cleveland Scholarship Program was about to begin, with applications limited to children in kindergarten through third grade. When the fax came through, while Roberta's main motivation was finding the right school for Tatiana, she put both of her youngest daughters' names on the application. She received a reply in the mail. "They said," Roberta recalls, "you can't do that. Each child is supposed to apply separately. Tatiana didn't get a voucher, but Toshika did."

"The problem was, Cedar Hill, the kids' school, wasn't in Cleveland, it was in Cleveland Heights," Roberta explains, and suburban schools were not eligible for the program. "So I couldn't use the voucher there. I checked into a Christian school called Second New Hope, and I ended up sending all five children there, Toshika on the voucher, and the other four on tuition, $700 per month, total. Financially, it made sense to keep them all together. That's the only way I could get a discount on the total tuition."

Second New Hope wasn't the kind of educational experience Roberta wanted for her children. "They just never seemed to have it together. I didn't think any of my kids were doing all that well there." Tatiana, in particular, found the adjustment difficult. "The teacher never called me to tell me. I would just come to school and find Tatiana standing in the hall outside her class," Roberta recalls. So when the year ended, Roberta looked into using Toshika's voucher to transfer her to St. John Nottingham, a Lutheran school not far from the Kitchen home. Roberta sent Toshika there, as well as Tatiana, Tiara, and DeAntye, while Tiffany enrolled at Collinwood in the Cleveland public school system.

While St. John seemed to work well for DeAntye, Tiara, and little Toshika, Tatiana was struggling again. "They called me in near the end of the year," says Roberta, "and basically asked Tatiana to leave. They told me they didn't have the in-school counselor they needed to help children like Tatiana, with her behavior problems."

Tatiana remained eligible for the Cleveland Scholarship Program, and Roberta kept trying to get her a voucher. "I kept sending in the application. And then finally I got a letter that she was chosen. That was a blessed day. I really didn't know what I was going to do. I knew that on my salary, each year the cost [of tuition] was going up, at some point it wouldn't work."

Suddenly, Roberta had educational options for Tatiana. The question was where to enroll her.

"About that time, I saw an article in the paper about a businessman named David Brennan. He had started new schools, two of them in Cleveland, and they were taking voucher students. I was reading what he was saying about education and I thought, 'I think like that.'" The HOPE schools initially enrolled kindergartners through third graders, and grew one grade each year as the children moved up. HOPE was offering a fifth grade class that fall.

"I belong to a group called the Institute for Black Family Development, out of Detroit. We had a core group, a bunch of us who had always talked about quitting what we were doing and starting a school. We had the vision," recalls Roberta. "We just had to get the training. That was what my education admin courses at Cleveland State were all about."

"Now, Brennan said in the article that he'd help anyone who wanted to start a school of their own. So I got the number of his office. My idea wasn't necessarily about Tatiana," says Roberta, "I wanted to see if he could help us start a school. I didn't get through, and I didn't pursue it, with all the other things going on." But Kitchen did pay a visit to the HOPE Academy, Brennan's East Side Choice school, operating out of an old Catholic grade school on East 55th Street.

"I went, really, with the idea of selling them on Tatiana," Kitchen remembers. "You know, this is a good girl, even though she doesn't always show it. I was ready to get up on my soapbox, even though I was getting so tired of selling these so-called high-risk children of mine," recounts Roberta, "trying to talk teachers into teaching them."

"But at HOPE, I didn't have to do that. I started in, and they just said, 'We'll take her.' Just like that. Tatiana was in."

"I won't say it's been easy. Tatiana became very well known in the principal's office. But every day is getting better. On a scale of one to ten she might be a four," says Roberta, "but that's excellent given where she's come from."

Roberta was certain she'd finally found the right school for Tatiana, but that wasn't to be the end of the difficult decisions she'd face. In the spring of Tatiana's fifth grade year, the Ohio Supreme Court struck down the Cleveland voucher program on procedural grounds; even as legislators in Columbus geared up to re-enact Cleveland's choice program before fall, the HOPE schools' administrators made a choice of their own: They would leave the voucher program, and convert to charter school status.

Roberta Kitchen sympathizes with the choice HOPE administrators had to make. "I know the [HOPE] administrators felt that if they continued with the vouchers, it would just be a never-ending battle. They felt they had to change, and get more stability that way. I knew that, by choosing to stay there, to keep Tatiana there, and because of that giving up the voucher, if HOPE doesn't go up to eighth grade, then I'm in a pickle." With no sibling preference policy, the fact that Toshika receives a voucher would not entitle Tatiana to one. "And even if Tatiana did get her voucher back," says Kitchen, "you're still left with the [private] schools on the list."

"With Tatiana," says Roberta, "there is so much there, if you only look hard enough to see it. But how many [schools] will want a D-average child like Tatiana, with all she's been through?" Roberta also worried about the continuing controversy that kept the Cleveland Scholarship Program on the front page and in the courts. "Every day in the paper, you could see the politics.

Three or four schools that took vouchers were in court, being challenged by the school system."

"What I like about HOPE is the fact that I'm able to go and talk to the teachers, and they listen. I think that's because we choose to be there. So in the end, I just felt I had to keep Tatiana where she was," says Kitchen, "and hope for the best."

• • •

FIFTEEN YEARS HAVE PASSED since Roberta's goddaughter went out for a pack of cigarettes and didn't return. In that time, Roberta and her children have forged a solid, functioning family unit, with the strength and security children need.

From the first, Roberta wanted to take the children in, but was concerned about how she'd make things work financially. In her conversations with county officials, recalls Roberta, "I said, 'I'll take them, but you have to help.'" The county provided medical coverage for all five children, in addition to "$100 for each child, each month, from AFDC," says Roberta. "For six months, that is. Then I went in for my regular 'redetermination,' and the payments stopped. They said my income counted against me."

For the past few years, the children have been on disability payments. All told, Roberta receives $251 per month for all five children.

"I never wanted foster parent status," explains Roberta. "That designation means they can come in and move the children. It's better to have guardianship. The county keeps coming at you, in my case, saying 'You're single.' I just kept saying that we were doing fine, there are plenty of single women raising families, you know. My view was just that they were not going to split the children up, put them in different homes." Roberta was patient and persistent; it paid off. "For Tiffany, DeAntye, and Tiara, the county gave me guardianship in 1985." After Tatiana and Toshika joined their siblings in Roberta's home, she was named guardian for them, too.

Roberta has "redetermination" meetings with the county every six months. "If I adopted them, we'd lose their medical coverage and their monthly payments, which aren't that much per child, but we need them." Another reason stands between Roberta and adoption: "To go that route, you would have to call the mother's fitness in doubt." That is something Roberta simply isn't willing to do.

• • •

ROBERTA KITCHEN SITS at her dining room table talking about the kind of education she wants for her children.

"At St. John and Lutheran East," DeAntye's private high school, "it's a traditional education they offer. I'm Christian, but not Lutheran. I like the fact that at St. John and Lutheran East the instructors know God, and the schools make a place for faith. But I'm looking at it in terms of values, consistency, and discipline," says Roberta. "A place that cares for the head and heart. That's what matters."

"Take Tiara. She has ADHD, so she has trouble concentrating. She can't take a test in a class with other children. She may know the answer, but she can't get to it. She's focused in on all the other things going on around her. So her teacher at St. John came up with a system to send her out to an empty room to take her tests. She can filter out the distractions. I appreciate that. I wouldn't even expect that, it would be unfair to expect that, in public schools."

Now with Tatiana, I'm not looking for tradition. I am looking for what works for each child: a way to reach kids who aren't making it, but who are able to. You know, a place where teachers are open to the idea of, '*study me. Find out how I learn.*' And then teach to that."

• • •

WITH TATIANA AT HOPE UNDER the charter program, and Toshika at St. John on a voucher, these days Roberta Kitchen has only two tuition bills to pay, for her son, DeAntye, and her daughter, Tiara. Together, DeAntye's and Tiara's tuition cost Roberta $633 per month.

I ask Roberta what she would do if Judge Oliver's decision to strike down the Cleveland Scholarship Program is upheld by higher courts.

"I'd take a second job, and if that wasn't enough, I would quit my job and home school them," says Roberta in a quiet voice. "Private school is what's giving my children a chance. I have invested too much to let [the public schools] turn my children into something that has a hole in it."

"You know, when I heard in the spring that the judge had ruled against the program, and I heard the [public] school system saying, 'Now all these kids are going to flood back into the system,' that was a lie."

"That was not an option," Kitchen says. "Not for me, not for any of the parents I talked to. They were talking about home school, or finding a way to pay. I think that ought to tell them something."

"There was a story not too long ago, about a grandmother in Euclid," an East Side suburb that borders the city of Cleveland. "She filed a false paper saying her grandkids lived with her to get them out of the Cleveland schools," says Roberta. "She got caught, and they were talking about jail time."

"It's just such an indictment of the public schools. If the public schools opened the doors tomorrow, they'd have a mass exodus. To say choice is the problem, it doesn't make sense."

"I have yet to understand what this court case is all about. It amazes me that this thing that can help so many has been made so complex. Religion? At ground level, [choice schools] are not promoting religion. It's just baloney," says Roberta. "We're not Lutheran, but Lutheran East is the right school for DeAntye, just like St. John is right for Tiara and Toshika. It just doesn't hold water. It just seems to be another way to hold back the people who need the help the most."

I ask Roberta if she ever feels she's abandoned the public schools. "You know, I really do want to see public schools get better," Roberta insists. "Even before I got my children, I've been involved in mentoring and counseling with city youth groups through the organization I belong to," says Roberta. "I've been in plenty of public schools. I remember one where I saw a room, it was like a holding room, filled with kids who were in in-school detention, they call it. It was a room full of young black boys." Kitchen shakes her head. "No chairs, no place to even ask them to sit and try to do some homework or read a book. Just a bunch of boys standing, milling around, waiting for the bell to ring. What kind of education is that?"

"And I think of all the parents who say, 'Well, at least my boy's going to school, he's not on the street.' They assume because their child is in school that he's being taught."

"I think of those boys, that this is the pool we're going to draw from for our future. What's happening to them—it's a kind of genocide. It's like there's a lack of hope hovering over the whole system."

"I guess I'm thinking of that now because not too long ago one of the local TV channels here played a tape of what was going on in one school," says Roberta, recalling video footage shot surreptitiously at Gallagher Middle School. The tape, which aired on Cleveland's local Fox network, "showed how nothing was going on," recalls Roberta. "Just chaos. No teachers teaching, just kids running wild."

"It's just too easy to make promises," Roberta says. "We have voted for levies, we have paid more and more and more and get less and less and less. We get a new superintendent who comes in with a new plan, stays for a year, and that's it. He's gone."

"One superintendent came in with her agenda—'Something or other 2000,'" Roberta recalls, shaking her head. "She was big on face-to-face dialogue with parents. They called a series of meetings around Cleveland, so when they were coming to the Collinwood/Wade Park cluster," Roberta's neighborhood, "I went. The superintendent wasn't even at the meeting! So much for face-to-face."

"Then there was the big parents' forum, 'Parents Count' or whatever," recalls Roberta. "It was a summit session on the public schools, downtown at the Cleveland Convocation Center. I went to that, too. I wanted to show, you know, to make change in the public schools, 'I am with this.'"

"When you got there, they had a big report, already bound, as thick as a phonebook. Excuse me!" marvels Roberta. "Of course, it had 'DRAFT' stamped on the front in big letters, but I had to wonder, what kind of comment would you have to make before they'd break into that and rewrite anything based on what a parent said?"

"It was business as usual," Kitchen concludes. "I was disappointed I fell for it."

"What I see is, the people running [the public schools] don't have any sense of urgency. As a parent, it's too late for you to say, 'Trust me. Give me time.' If my children are already in school, I don't have time to give you."

Roberta Kitchen leans across her dining room table to make her point. "I want to say to them, 'Tell me, which child of mine should I sacrifice?'"

Chapter Three

SAN ANTONIO

SAN ANTONIO

SINCE 1992, SAN ANTONIO has been the site of one of the first privately funded school choice programs in the country, the San Antonio CEO (Children's Educational Opportunities) Program. Patterned after Indianapolis' Charitable Choice Trust, begun in 1991, and similar in program design to Milwaukee's PAVE program, San Antonio CEO served 926 children in its first year, offering half-scholarships averaging $565, with a cap regardless of total tuition of $700. For the 1999–2000 school year, San Antonio CEO provided 724 students from low-income families half-tuition grants averaging $1,098 to attend the school of their choice.[9] Interest in the program far outstrips available resources; San Antonio CEO's waiting list numbers 1,832 children.

To qualify for a CEO grant, families must meet the same guidelines for the federal free-or-reduced price lunch program, which in 1999-2000 was a maximum income of $30,433 for a family of four. The average income of San Antonio CEO families is far lower: $16,553.[10]

In 1998, the success of San Antonio CEO spawned the Horizon Program, a novel experiment backed by a $50-million, ten-year commitment to offer vouchers to low-income parents across an entire public school district, in this

---

[9] Kindergarten through eighth grade grants are capped at $1,000, while ninth through twelfth grade grants can be as much as $1,500.

[10] Teresa Treat, executive director, San Antonio CEO, telephone interview, March 30, 2000.

instance, the Edgewood Independent School District on San Antonio's west side. The population of Edgewood is 98 percent Hispanic, and overwhelmingly low-income, with an average family income of $15,816 and more than half of all residents living below the poverty line. For Hispanic students, the dropout rate from Edgewood's public schools is 60 percent.[11]

Established as a form of what program director Robert Aguirre calls "shock treatment" to a failing public school system, the impact of Horizon was immediate. In the program's first year, 1998–1999, 837 students in the Edgewood ISD used Horizon vouchers to attend 57 private schools across the city. Horizon vouchers are worth $3,600 per child for students enrolled in kindergarten through eighth grade, and $4,000 per child for students enrolled in ninth through twelfth grade. While receiving schools are free to screen incoming students according to their usual application procedures, in practice, only eight of the 57 schools do, leaving 49 schools that accept any student who chooses to attend.

Given that the Horizon experiment was financed through private funds and not public means, voucher opponents have had no legal or legislative avenues of attack against the San Antonio program. Nevertheless, stung by the program's open invitation to low-income families to abandon the public schools, the public education establishment mounted its bully pulpit to question the program's purpose. According to the Texas Federation of Teachers, Horizon would "shorten the honor roll" in public schools, by creaming off their best and brightest students. As Dolores Muñoz, superintendent of the Edgewood ISD, put it: "I guarantee you that at least 80 percent will be the high-achieving students. The private schools are having the choice of the best students around…. Their doors are…not open to every child." After two years, Horizon is only now beginning to generate achievement data that allows an assessment of its classroom impact. Even now, however, it is possible to assess the accuracy of voucher opponents' predictions that the program would siphon the best and brightest inner city students out of the public schools, and pronounce those fears unfounded. For example, 23 percent of

[11] According to Robert Aguirre, Managing Director of CEO Horizon (CEO America Conference, Grand Rapids, Michigan, May 17, 2000).

Horizon students had been in Gifted and Talented programs in their public school compared with 29 percent of the overall Edgewood ISD student body, while voucher students and public school students were equally as likely to have been suspended during the past school year.[12]

[12.] Paul E. Peterson, David Myers and William G. Howell, "An Evaluation of the Horizon Scholarship Program in the Edgewood Independent School District, San Antonio, Texas: The First Year," Harvard Program on Education Policy and Governance, September 1999, p. 3.

San Antonio CEO Program
FIRST YEAR IN OPERATION: 1992-93

Eligibility:
- 185% of federal free or reduced price lunch program
- Resident of Bexar County
- Awards made on first-come basis

Value of voucher:
- Half tuition, to a maximum of $1,000 for grades 1–8 and $1,500 for grades 9–12
- Parents provide the remainder
- Vouchers averaged $1,098 per student for 1999–2000 year

Current participation:
- 654 students at 92 schools for the 2000–2001 year
- 1,832 students on waiting list

San Antonio Horizon Program
FIRST YEAR IN OPERATION: 1998–99

Eligibility:
- Resident of the Edgewood (Public) Independent School District
- All eligible students previously attending public schools may be awarded scholarships as they apply
- Students previously attending a private school are awarded scholarships by lottery on a 15:1 ratio (For every 15 public school students awarded a scholarship, 1 student from the private list is awarded a scholarship by lottery.)

Value of voucher:

For private schools within Edgewood ISD:
- $3,600 for K–8 students for 1999–2000 year
- $4,000 for grades 9–12 students

For public or private schools outside Edgewood ISD:
- Up to $2,000 for K–8 students
- Up to $3,500 for grades 9–12 students

Current participation:
- 1,321 students at 64 schools for the 2000–2001 year

Leroy and Hattie Batts with their grandson, Kevin.

LEROY BATTS

"Maybe the reason I'm here is because
I have reason to be."

LEROY BATTS SITS with his angular arms folded on the oilcloth-covered kitchen table, trying to recall when the first warning signs came from his grandson Kevin's school. "Second grade is when we really knew. I mean, Kevin's been a slow-burner all along," says Batts. "But second grade is when his teacher called and told us he was really having a hard time keeping up, and he ought to be put into special ed." Batts and his wife, Hattie, had wondered as much themselves; the teacher and the Battses raised the issue with school administrators at San Antonio's Lyndon Baines Johnson Elementary, "but there wasn't a lot of interest there," recalls Leroy. "We waited, but nothing happened. So finally Kevin's teacher did the paperwork herself, so he could get the special ed tutoring she thought he needed."

"It was hard on the boy. You know how kids are cruel. Kevin got the special ed tutoring on Tuesdays and Thursdays, I think it was," Batts recalls, looking over at his wife Hattie to confirm his recollection. "It singles a kid out. He's got the other kids calling him 'dummy' and such. But he did need the extra instruction, because the tutoring helped, no question."

"The problem was the way he'd bounce in and out of the tutoring," Leroy continues. "He'd get the extra time, and his grades would improve. Then they'd take him off tutoring because he'd caught up with the class, and his marks would drop." Batts's hands trace the arc of an aircraft in a death dive. "It was up and down, up and down, fluctuating the whole time he was at

LBJ, and Wrenn, too [Kevin's junior high]. They'd mainstream him, he'd slip, then they'd put him back in special ed. We're looking at D's and F's when he's on his own," recalls Leroy Batts, "and back up to C's when he's got the tutor."

"Overall, his grades were middling. Nothing bad enough to hold him back. I think they were passing him to justify the program," opined Batts. "It's not to say my grandson was some sort of babbling idiot. That's not it. But the plain truth is, he didn't have it together. He just didn't, plain for anyone to see."

"Physically, he was mainstreamed, right there in the regular classroom, with every other kid," says Batts. "But administratively, he was special ed, so [the school] got the extra funds that come along with that. You know how it is: The name of the game is money."

"You know though, what really got me upset was the label. To get the assistance he needed under the public school system, they had to put a label on Kevin of 'emotionally disturbed, emotionally unstable.'" Leroy Batts pauses, palms flat on the table top. "All these years, and that still upsets me."

At one point when Kevin's school had withdrawn his special ed tutoring, Leroy Batts had his grandson privately tested, using his own insurance coverage. "They told me he has ADD," says Leroy. "Not with hyperactivity, just the inability to concentrate. I know they're seeing ADD everywhere these days, but Kevin's got it. Read up on it as much as I have, and it's a textbook case."

If Kevin's problems are deep-seated, their source is no mystery. When he was three years old, Kevin Batts witnessed the murder of his mother, at the hands of a man Leroy Batts describes as "a crack cocaine fiend, a real dope addict." Leroy and Hattie Batts have been raising their grandson ever since.

I ask Leroy Batts whether Kevin's father is in any way part of his son's life. "No," says Leroy, "he's not. He's in jail, serving a life sentence for murder."

• • •

LEROY BATTS IS 68; his wife, Hattie, Leroy says with a husband's courtly circumspection, "is around that age herself." Retired now, Batts talks about a 22-year Air Force career in which he saw duty in Vietnam at Cam Ranh Bay with the 12th Fighter Wing, "and Korea, too," he continues, "but not actually in Korea, because I was on the airbase over in Japan." Leroy Batts is content that his globe-traveling days are over. Hattie Batts has a lung disease, emphysema, brought on by a heavy smoking habit, and takes pure oxygen through a nasal tube when she's at home. Hattie sits on the couch, along a wall of tropical fish tanks, near her breathing apparatus, while Leroy Batts and I sit at the kitchen table, talking about what it's like to raise a teenage boy at an age when most of his Air Force contemporaries, says Batts with his customary directness, are "already dead."

"I've always been one to stay busy, stay active. When I retired from the service, I liked tinkering with cars," recalls Leroy, "so I took a job at an auto parts store. The fellas I served with, most of them retired and did nothing. A few years ago, I was thinking of the group of buddies I served with. If you can believe it, I'm the only one still alive."

"Maybe the reason I'm here," Batts says with a wry smile, "is because I have reason to be."

The Battses' six children range from 35 to 43 years old; they have five grandchildren and two great-grandchildren. In addition to losing Kevin's mother, Leroy and Hattie Batts's second daughter is also deceased, having succumbed to a brain tumor more than two decades earlier. "That's why we settled here in San Antonio," Leroy explains. "Lackland [Air Force Base] was the best Air Force medical facility to treat our daughter. She didn't make it, but we stayed."

The only other family Kevin has is a 25-year-old brother. Leroy Batts is vague as to what Kevin's brother does, other than to say he's in a rehabilitation program, and "drops by from time to time." "It would be wonderful for Kevin to have a big brother who played that role," says Leroy. "But as it is,

[Kevin] is the one who's got the sense his brother just doesn't have." Kevin Batts is at track practice as we speak. "Don't let Kevin hear me say that," says Leroy Batts. "Kevin," says his grandfather, "won't abide anything negative being said about his brother."

For the first time, Hattie Batts enters the conversation: "Not that [Kevin]'s not making judgments, mind you. Kevin sees his brother's problems. Kevin's right there, telling him, 'You shouldn't be doing what you're doing.' Kevin kicks him in the leg. You should see it."

"Which doesn't stop him from laying into me the other day for telling his brother that very same thing," says Leroy Batts.

• • •

LEROY AND HATTIE BATTS LIVE in the house they bought in 1969 on West Commerce Street, five years before Leroy took his retirement. Standing under the carport, where he's got the hood up on his vintage 1974 Buick Electra "deuce and a quarter"—"when I've got her washed and waxed and I take her out, she still turns heads," he says—Leroy Batts gestures towards the streaking traffic: "No two ways about it, this neighborhood's gone downhill. It used to be, up and down this street there were Air Force families, people stationed at Lackland or Kelly Air Force Base," recalls Leroy. "Now, it's pretty much a ghetto. Things that never happened here 30 years ago happen now, in broad daylight."

Batts's words remind me of the scene I witnessed just minutes before, driving to his home. Around the corner on General McMullen Avenue, police had four youths spread-eagled against a squad car. Anywhere else, an arrest in progress might generate a crowd of gawkers. The tableau certainly attracted my attention, but I noticed several people at a bus stop on the same side of the street, straining to see past the police car. They seem to be looking for their bus, caught in traffic, as one lane squeezes past the police car. In Batts's West Commerce neighborhood, an arrest is a just a minor annoyance that can make a bus late.

Statistics bear out Leroy's assessment of a neighborhood fallen on hard times. According to U.S. Census data, 60 percent of all adults in Batts's neighborhood failed to earn a high school diploma; nearly a third did not attend school past the eighth grade. While the percentage of people living below the poverty line is nearly 40 percent, for children 11 or under, the percentage rises to 50 percent and more. Nearly two-thirds of all homes are owner-occupied, with a median value of $32,400. Per capita income in 1990 was $5,570— about one-fourth the U.S. average.[13]

• • •

"HERE'S THE THING ABOUT KEVIN," says Leroy Batts, "and I guess about ADD kids in general: They hate change." Batts explains that for a child with ADD, even something as routine as cleaning up his cluttered room can cause anxiety. "I start with the reminders about a week or ten days ahead. No surprises," says Batts. "I tell him, Kevin, we're going to get after that room of yours. Then, when the day comes, I bring that 30-gallon trashcan and set it right in the middle of his room, and we just go through things together. He says he's fine about it, but I can see how nervous and agitated it gets him."

Kevin Batts sees a therapist, the same one for nearly a decade. "She's wonderful," says Leroy. "It is really important for Kevin to have someone he can talk to, not me or his grandmother, about whatever is weighing on his mind," says Batts. "And she's seen him so long now, she's really just a part of his life. Kevin sees her several times a month. Well that's how often it used to be," Leroy corrects himself. "She seems to be trying to wean him away now, so it's maybe every three weeks."

"You've got to understand. Kevin doesn't like change, no change of any sort. His therapist moved her office once. Kevin went to see her at the new place and he came out all shook up. He told me, 'Granddaddy, I told her to never do that to me again.'"

13. U.S. Census microsample, obtained from the University of Wisconsin Applied Population Lab.

"You know, Kevin's come a long way from where he was. I can tell you when it was we knew he needed help. Kevin was no more than four, he'd been with us about a year. My sister had a stroke. She was paralyzed, and she came to live with us. We set her up in one of the bedrooms," Leroy remembers. "Kevin just didn't like it, couldn't get used to the fact my sister was here, even though she's paralyzed, confined to her bed. I mean, you're in the rest of the house, you don't even know she's here."

"Well, one night, my wife and I were in bed. We smelled smoke. It was coming from the room my sister was in. Kevin had gone in there with a pack of matches, and set her bedsheet on fire," Batts recalls. "We got the fire out, and everything was okay. But that's when we knew Kevin needed to see somebody who could help him get stable, and deal with the world around him."

Hattie Batts leaves the room. Leroy leans in. "You know, Kevin saw the whole thing with his mother, right up 'til the end. He can tell you he watched her arms thrashing, thrashing, and then she got completely still. For all the time he's been with us, he's had dreams, nights when he'd roll around in bed so hard you could hear his arms and legs hitting the wall."

"It's not happening so much any more, I think now that school's evening out. But you know, growing up for these kids these days is a challenge in itself without all the stuff Kevin's got to deal with."

• • •

"THE ONE THING I WON'T EVER FORGET from all those years is the [special ed] conferences they hold for the parents," says Leroy Batts. "I mean, they move 'em through like cattle. You'd see the parents sitting there, going in one after the other. Five minutes, that's all, they're in and out." Batts shakes his head. "My time comes, I'd push for some information, and I'd get 10 minutes, twice what anyone else got, but nothing in the way of information that really told us anything about what's going on for Kevin."

One time, Kevin's therapist told Leroy she'd like to come to the next school conference. "She's got a masters in social work. She's a great lady, been seeing Kevin since not too long after we took him. She knows him better than anyone, and it was her idea to go," Batts recalls. "She thought it would help the school specialists to know something about Kevin's history."

Leroy called the school to tell them Kevin's therapist would be attending the next session. "When we got there, you couldn't believe it. They brought in more officials. The principal was there, someone from the superintendent's office was there, the heavy artillery," Batts laughs. "It was like they had to outnumber us."

"You know, Kevin's therapist is also an ex-school teacher. She really could relate in every way to what the school was dealing with," says Batts. "But every time she made a comment, there was silence. No response. Like they had been told not to engage her in any sort of conversation, just deny her existence, like she wasn't even there."

It was a familiar scene for Leroy and Hattie Batts. "All along, their attitude was, 'Mr. Batts, you're just a layperson. What could you know?'"

"Now, in the service, I was a mental health technician. That's what I trained for. So at one of Kevin's meetings, I told them, 'I'm not a professional, but I'm in tune with what's going on here.' I mean, I know the terminology," says Leroy, "and what's going on behind all the big words."

"It didn't matter. They could care less what I might know about Kevin."

• • •

I ASK LEROY BATTS WHAT KEVIN'S transition from LBJ Elementary to Wrenn Junior High was like. "Rocky," sighs Leroy. "That's when the problems really began."

"I never did get a good feeling from Wrenn. There's gangs there, graffiti and all the like," says Batts. "Of course the administrators there, they're all in denial. When Kevin was in sixth grade, we went to a function at Wrenn for kids who would be coming up to seventh grade the next year. We went on a little tour of the building, and between the time we went around back and came back out front, there was gang grafitti spray-painted on the building!"

"Another time, not too long after Kevin got there, I was sitting in the hall-way. I was a little early I guess for one of our meetings on Kevin's situation. There were teachers running around with two-way radios in their hands," Batts recalls, "and they were yelling at these kids in the halls. It was like something out of state prison, not junior high school. I mean, screaming at a child, right in his face: Young minds shouldn't have to experience that sort of thing."

Yet what most alarmed Leroy Batts was the amount of fighting Kevin was drawn into at Wrenn. Kevin, a large boy for his age, with a smooth, round face and a gentle demeanor, "got beat up pretty bad, twice."

"We'd be home in the afternoon, and I'd pick up the phone extension in [the kitchen] to make a call. Kevin would be on with a kid, booking a fight after school," says Leroy, "like a fight promoter. Next day, Kevin would come home all banged up."

"And this is supposed to be his friend," Batts shakes his head.

"One day he came home with his eye swollen shut. It was so bad I took Kevin to see his pediatrician. He thought his eye-socket was cracked. But the X-rays came out negative, and the eye healed up, though it's still not right. If you look at it, it still wanders a little bit."

"That was the straw that broke the camel's back," says Leroy. "I called the school, and scheduled an appointment with the vice-principal. When I got there, she kept me waiting. Then finally, her door opened and she walked right past me and out of the office," Batts recalls. "I know she saw me, and I know the secretary had told her I was there. I followed her out into the hall, and she must have had second thoughts, walking by me like that. She turned around, and we talked."

"But that was it, right there in the hall. Like she was too busy to see me in her office. I thought for something that serious," Leroy continues, "that was wrong. I wasn't demanding. I wasn't insulting or confrontational."

Batts returned to the office and asked to see the principal. "He was aware of what had happened to Kevin. So I asked him, what are you going to do about this?"

"He said, 'Mr. Batts, we're thinking alternative.'" Leroy Batts' hands flutter up in disbelief. "Alternative school, that's his answer, not just for the guys doing this to Kevin, but for Kevin, too. So when they're starting to talk about moving him to an alternative school, that's when we started looking for ways to move him out."

Batts went home and called Kevin's therapist. "I figured I'd ask her to help me find a good private school for Kevin. Of course, tuition was the other part of the problem. We started looking around. They were quoting me $500, $600 a month [for tuition]," Leroy recalls. "One school was $950 a month. My wife and I knew we'd have to tighten our belts, let some things go to afford it. But with the dollars they were talking about, it wasn't looking good."

Around that time, Leroy's daughter-in-law told him about New Life Christian Academy, a school on San Antonio's North Side, about ten minutes from the Batts home on West Commerce. "Even there, it was $150 per month. I don't know how they got it that low, but we were still scrambling to put aside even that much."

It was the summer before Kevin's eighth grade year. "Then one day the mail came and I found this letter. Something about a Horizon program, for kids like Kevin in the Edgewood district."

"It was God-sent," says Batts. "I filled out the application that same day, and sent it in. A few days later we got a letter back, saying Kevin could get his tuition paid. No time at all."

The Battses contacted New Life. "I told them, we've got a Horizon scholarship, and that's where we want Kevin come next fall."

• • •

"FUNNY THING WAS," recalls Batts, "hard as it was to get anyone to pay attention to us all the time Kevin was in public school, when we got on Horizon, they just couldn't seem to let us go."

"I went to Wrenn and told them Kevin wouldn't be back, and I needed his records sent to his new school." The transfer was of even greater importance given Kevin's challenges and the many evaluations in his file. "I signed the release form to have the records sent, but New Life called and said they hadn't come."

"So I went back. The people at Wrenn sent me to an Edgewood board building to sign another release. When I got there, they asked me, 'Why did you come? Who sent you here?' Still, I signed a release form there, and still no records. And now, the school year's starting, and New Life is telling me I've got to get those records there."

"So a few days later, I went back to Kevin's school. Now, there's a new problem: Kevin owed the school for a science book he hadn't turned in. Why they didn't come up with that one in the first place, I don't know. Now the school never had enough books to go around, and Kevin shared a science book all year with another kid. So how they know that even if it is lost that Kevin lost it—I don't know that either. But I figured I've got to pay," says Leroy. He was told he owed $30.

"And you know, they wouldn't take a check, like I was going to skip town, not just transfer Kevin. So I went home and got cash."

"That's when I started to notice how stirred up the Edgewood people were about this new Horizon program. Every day, I started to notice the newspaper stories, and the things the Edgewood teachers and principals were saying. Some of the articles said none of the kids transferring out would make it in private school. They'd all come crawling back [to public school]. Then the next day, they'd change gears. The private schools were bad because they didn't have accreditation, they weren't certified like public schools were."

"But the one I liked best of all," Batts recalls with a smile, "was how the private schools were taking the 'cream of the crop.'"

• • •

Hard by Lackland Air Force Base, above the roar of San Antonio's Highway 90, rises the ruddy red brick building that houses New Life Christian Academy. In the parking lot, a stylized metal butterfly crowns a stadium-style message board. The flashing message, large enough to be seen by the speeding motorists on Highway 90, reads:

Bible Study...
Family Prayer Nite...
1:14 p.m. 76 degrees.
Come Worship With Us!

Leroy Batts describes the difference he's seen since Kevin started at New Life. "Mind you, it's been tough for Kevin. As bad as Wrenn was, as often as he was getting beat on by the other kids," Batts recalls, "Kevin didn't want to change schools. He'd just come up to Wrenn from LBJ the year before. It was too much change for him to cope with. If we'd have let him, he'd have stayed."

Still, Leroy is confident New Life is the right school for Kevin. "They don't have a label on him. There is no LD or special ed designation," says Batts. "I suspect they deal with a lot of ADD kids up there, and they just know what to expect and how to deal with them."

"Kevin's on Ritalin for the ADD," says Leroy, who reads up on Kevin's medications, as well as his own and his wife Hattie's via the WebTV hookup he bought at the base PX for $39. "It was the old system, they were looking to clear them out when the new ones came out. I figured that's about right for me. So yes, I'm on the Internet," says Batts with a laugh. "Just don't ask me to run my big-screen TV, though. That's Kevin's job."

"You know, in all the brochures and the booklets from the school, they're not putting themselves forth as an ADD facility or anything. In fact, I don't think there's any mention of special education."

"But they seem to know ADD when they see it. And that's a big help, that alone. They're not looking at the behavior in a negative manner, just how to deal with it to allow the learning to take place. They have a handle on it, on the behavior, and how to work around it."

"I used to get notes from Kevin's old school all the time, nastygrams, I call 'em," recalls Leroy. "Kevin's locker is a disaster, it would say. Well, okay,

ADD kids," Batts continues, "they can't stand throwing anything away. Real packrats. So his locker's a mess. Tell me something new!"

"At New Life, the principal tells me once every few weeks, he says, 'Kevin, time to clean out your locker,' and he walks down with him and stands there," says Batts with a smile, "pretty much like we do at home. And Kevin cleans out his locker."

"At Wrenn, Kevin said he'd say to the teacher, 'I can't understand this.' And they'd tell him, 'If you can't understand it, read it.' At New Life, Kevin tells me, 'When that happens, Granddaddy, the teacher stands right by you and works with you until you do understand.'"

"They're strict. That's true. But there's no yelling and screaming at him like there was before."

"I'm not saying that Kevin's any kind of choir boy. Just the other week, he was in a fist fight. Some boys in class were shooting rubber bands back and forth, the teacher stepped out of the room for a moment and it escalated from there. I went in to the school to meet with the teacher. He had Kevin there," says Batts. "I liked that. We weren't behind closed doors talking about him, him outside wondering what was going on. We all kind of realized the hormones are flying for boys this age. Not to condone it—we didn't—but not to make more of it than it was."

"So we sorted things out, and Kevin said he shook hands with the boy the next day. I don't expect they're fast friends or anything, but I think it's over with. And that's a good way to handle these things. The school seems on top of it."

• • •

TALK TO KEVIN BATTS, and you will hear more "yes sirs" and "no sirs" in a few minutes than for months at a time before or after. I ask him to tell me about New Life. "Nice teachers. Good teams," says Kevin in a quiet voice. "I like to play a lot of sports. I play forward in basketball. I play guard and tackle in football, and I play baseball and throw the shotput in track." Because New Life fields a unified varsity football team, Kevin even played in some varsity games as a freshman. When I comment that that's quite an accomplishment, Kevin sets me straight. "We didn't have too many seniors this year," he says by way of explanation.

I ask Kevin if there are any classes that give him problems. "Math," he answers without hesitation. "I'm not all that good in it," he says with a directness he seems to have inherited from his grandfather. Even so, Kevin is careful to tell me he's getting between a 73 and 75 in math, "that's a C, and in science I have a 90."

I ask Kevin what things were like at his old junior high. "It was different. One day, the guys will be your friend," says Kevin, "the next day, not. They'll be talking behind your back and all that."

I push him to tell me something he liked at Wrenn. "Computer class. Our teacher let us fool around sometimes, and if we got our work done, she let us play computer games." I ask Kevin if there's anything he misses about his old school. "No sir, that's pretty much it."

• • •

I ASK LEROY BATTS ABOUT THE RELIGIOUS element at New Life, and how it weighed into the decision about where to send Kevin to school. "I'm an agnostic," begins Leroy, explaining that he was brought up a Baptist in South Carolina. "It's not that I don't believe, just that I don't believe in any organized religion." The Battses don't belong to any church, nor does Kevin.

"I like the way New Life handles religion. Naturally, it's a Christian school. They teach the Bible. And the bulk of kids at New Life are from that church. But they don't push it on Kevin, that it's the one true way, or any of that. The way they approach it is, it's the Bible, let's see what it says. That's their approach. And that's beautiful to me."

• • •

WHEN LEROY BATTS TALKS about his grandson's future, he resists the wish projections parents typically make about their child's occupation or education or even marriage and family. What Leroy wishes for his grandson is simply a future in which Kevin is an independent adult. "Hattie and I were talking about that very thing this morning. I had just come back from dropping Kevin at school, and she said 'Do you think he's going to have to be led around by the hand for the rest of his life?'"

"And I said to Hattie, wait a minute: Think about how he used to be. I see a change, a big change. He stands up for himself. He's got more maturity. Even when he got in that fight at school, he showed some guts, some nerve. Not too long ago, with kids picking on him, Kevin would have gone into the corner and cried."

"My biggest worry is that this boy is too trusting," says Leroy. "Everyone's his friend. Of course, when you find out down the line they're not, the walls come falling in. Right now, when the walls fall in, we're there for Kevin. But what about when we're not?"

"With a good support system, he'll make it. I just hope he can find that support somewhere."

"I talked to Kevin about New Life, talked to him a lot when he first started in there. I asked him how he liked it. I still ask him every once in a while," says Batts.

"And you know what he says? Kevin tells me they treat him like a human. Isn't that something to say?" asks Leroy. "Now, if you think that says something about where he is now," Batts continues, "think about what it says about the school he used to be in."

At New Life, "he's got mostly B's. A C, maybe a C+ in math, a 76 I think last time. I say to Kevin, 'Hey that's great. We're not striving for perfection here. I just want you to pass, buddy.'"

"The thing I see is, he feels he's learning. And that's new. For school to be a positive, that's something new for Kevin."

The Alvarez family, (left to right) Marcos, Rosa, Myra, Juan, and Mariano, outside their San Antonio home.

JUAN ALVAREZ

"The seed is planted. There will be fruit."

JUAN ALVAREZ KNEW BY LOOKING at his son that something was wrong. Marcos had been acting odd, out of sorts, since coming home from school the day before. Now, in the morning, he announced to his father and mother he didn't want to go to school.

Marc, as his son liked to be called, was nine years old then, a second grader at Nelson Elementary School, directly across the street from the Alvarez home on the sun-scorched streets of West San Antonio. Juan and his wife, Rosa, had liked the fact that their boys attended school so close to the house, and Juan recalls peering out the living room window some afternoons to see if he could spot his boys playing during gym or recess. Lately, however, both his boys, not only Marcos but also his twin brother Mariano, had been getting into confrontations with other boys at Nelson. Juan Alvarez insisted that Marcos tell him if there was a problem at school.

"Finally, [Marcos] told me," Juan recalls. "He said he was in the library, looking for a book. Two kids came over to him, and one of the boys pulled his own pants down. They said things to Marc that weren't right."

"My son said, 'These kids, they give me a hard time,'" Juan remembers. "He say, 'Dad, I am a boy.' You see, he wanted to fight back. But we raise ourselves as Christians: No fighting, no cursing. He wanted to fight, but he knew he should not. Now he didn't want to go to school anymore."

Alvarez talked to school officials, but was unsatisfied with their response. "They said, 'It's just kids being kids. They were playing around,'" Juan recalls. "But that's not how it sounded to me. I knew something very wrong had happened."

"So then I went to [Marcos'] teacher, and I asked him what was going on." The teacher denied any immediate knowledge about the incident involving Marcos, but he didn't say that Juan Alvarez's fears were unfounded. "If I be you, he said, I'd take my kids out," recalls Juan. "That's what he said: If I be you, that's what I'd do."

Juan left the school unsure of what to do next. He decided to talk to someone at Faith Outreach, a Christian church that also ran a school. "I talked to the principal at Faith Outreach," says Alvarez. "I told him what happened. I said to him, I know it costs money, but I have to get my boys out."

"He talked to me about the CEO program," the privately funded San Antonio Children's Educational Opportunities Program that since 1992 had been providing partial grants to low-income San Antonio families seeking to send their children to private school. "I said, 'I don't know anything about it. Could they help me out?' But he said, 'Juan, getting in would be difficult.' There was a waiting list for the CEO, a thousand children, I think."

"I said, what will we do? We don't have that kind of money."

Alvarez went home. "My wife was very upset, almost ready to have a nervous breakdown. I had to do something." He sat down and wrote a letter to San Antonio CEO:

> *It is imperative and urgent that I write to you because of a problem that exists concerning some students, and our sons Marcos and Mariano Alvarez. It has my wife and me very disturbed.*
>
> *Some students are harassing Marcos and calling him names such as "queer," and he has become very depressed. Because of our Chris-*

tian faith, my children are not allowed to talk back, much less fight back. At one point, one student pulled his trousers down and exposed himself. This is intolerable, embarrassing, and very alarming.

I would like to discuss this matter with you as soon as possible. If there is a possibility that I can send my sons to a Christian school, through the CEO (Children's Educational Opportunity) Foundation, I would appreciate your assistance.

Sincerely,
Thank you very much,
[signed] Juan Alvarez

• • •

"SO I MAILED THE LETTER," Alvarez recalls. "And I prayed. I said, God, you've helped me so many times. They said when I got hurt, I wouldn't make it," says Juan, recalling the time several years earlier when doctors warned him that a nerve injury to his spine might paralyze him. "They said I would be a vegetable. But here I am, God," Alvarez reaches out upstretched arms. "Help us now."

A week went by. San Antonio CEO called. The news was better than even Juan and Rosa had hoped. The Alvarezes would indeed receive tuition assistance, not only for Marc and Mariano, but for the Alvarezes' eighth grade daughter, Myra, as well.

"My letter," says Alvarez, "went to the heart."

• • •

Sitting in the living room of the home he and Rosa bought seven years ago, Juan Alvarez recalls the concerns he had about his sons' public school. "You know, here's one thing: My sons, they stopped doing homework. I asked them, where are your books? What do you have to do tonight? And they say to me, we don't have any homework." Alvarez asked at the school, and the teacher told him his sons were telling the truth: He had been assigning less homework. "So many parents were complaining to him they were sitting too long at night doing homework with their kids," says Alvarez, shaking his head. "It didn't seem right to make that a reason to stop the homework. I don't care about the other parents. I didn't like that."

Then there was the picture Marc brought home early in second grade, a self portrait he had drawn at school. "He had a scarf across his mouth, like a gang outlaw. His face had scars on here and here," Juan Alvarez pulls his fingers across his cheeks. "Like in the gangs, the street-fighters, who are all the time cutting each other up with knives."

"That kind of a picture will open the eyes of a father," Juan recalls. "When I saw it, I started crying. I said, 'No, my son. You're not him. That boy isn't you,'" says Alvarez. "You see, what was in his heart was what he was drawing on that page."

"I told him, I hope one day I am going to show you a different picture. Not this one."

Even before the incident in the library involving Marcos, Juan and Rosa were afraid things would only get worse. "Drugs," says Alvarez, "that is my big worry." The Alvarezes knew that drugs were a problem in the upper grades, even in elementary schools. Whether that was true at Nelson, they weren't sure, but it was certainly an issue in junior high. Nor were the Alvarezes' concerns confined to Marcos and Mariano. They also had misgivings about the school their daughter Myra attended.

"I started having problems with her, too," says Juan, sitting in a well-worn easy chair in the Alvarez living room. "The way she was wearing baggy pants, bad language, bad grades. I'm a person who was raised by my grandparents. I'm not too strict, not as strict as my grandparents, that's for sure, but on education, yes, I am. I tell my children, your education, it's not for me, it's for you. I say, if they want jobs and opportunities, it's them, not me, that [must] do the work."

Myra Alvarez was an eighth grader at San Antonio's Horace Mann Junior High. "I was thinking she was in the wrong crowd at that school," says Juan. "So when the CEO said they could help, I wanted to move Myra to a new school as well."

The idea didn't sit well with Juan and Rosa's daughter. "Myra didn't want to go. She says, 'Just no. I'm staying. That's it,'" Alvarez recalls.

For a week, Myra fought to stay at her old school. Finally, Juan told her if she'd simply visit Faith Outreach, it would be her choice. "I said, just go, and you decide," recalls Juan. "I said, what you do is up to you."

Myra Alvarez remembers it a bit differently. "That's what my dad told you?" she asks. "My dad did say it was my choice, but I saw how he was when CEO said we'd get help. I didn't see how I could say no," says Myra. "We were driving in the car when my dad told me, and I just busted out crying. It was eighth grade, and all I could think of was the eighth grade prom coming up, and we were going to go on a class trip to Austin, the first time our school ever did that. And now I'd be missing out."

"He said I was mad?" Myra asks. "I hated my dad for that! I didn't talk to him all that week." Still, she went to Faith Outreach and toured the school; "I wasn't going to be rude," says Myra. Against her own inclinations, she had to admit she liked the school. She went home and told her father she would transfer.

• • •

JUAN ALVAREZ NEVER FINISHED high school in his hometown of Nuevo Laredo, Mexico. At eighteen, he came to the United States. For nearly

20 years, Juan worked a variety of jobs, starting out as a surveyor in Laredo, Texas, just across the border, moving to San Antonio where he worked as an insurance salesman with a staff under him and later as a waiter and then headwaiter in a series of Hilton Hotel restaurants. Then in 1980, Rosa became pregnant with their first child. At the age of 38, Juan Alvarez started thinking about going back to school to get his GED.

"I needed it for my job. You know, the applications all ask, 'do you have your high school diploma?' If you want to move to a higher level, you needed it." Juan took the GED prep course at San Antonio College. He took the GED test there, and passed.

"It was easy," he recalls, with evident pride. "I studied, took the test and that was it." For a year after, Juan took courses on and off at San Antonio College. I ask him why he stopped. "I had to work," says Alvarez. "So now I say to my kids, you go to school, and you stay in school."

"Mariano wants to go to college. He talks about it. Marc, he's not sure. I say, education is the best thing for kids. Try to set a goal. First high school, then college. When they say, hey, there's a nice car, I say, you want to pay for a car like that, you can't do it with a job as a laborer. You need education."

For the past ten years, Juan Alvarez has been unable to work, disabled by a nerve injury affecting his spine. "I always worked," says Juan, "even if my back, my neck had pain. You don't go to the doctor, you go to work. That is the way it is."

The disability lawyer Alvarez contacted asked him, "Juan, are you 'macho man?' You never went to the doctor. You just kept going to work. Now they don't have a record of how hurt you are." Doctors warned Juan that he risked paralysis if he kept working. He stopped, and now carries only the lightest loads.

Most days, volunteer work now occupies Juan Alvarez. In the afternoons, he makes the rounds at local restaurants, gleaning food for the poorest of San Antonio's poor. Every few weeks, he takes the old family van, laden with second-hand clothes, bread, and other food collected by the church, and sometimes by Juan, from his restaurant friends, south across the Mexican border to towns like Campeche, Veracruz, and even Oaxaca, a grueling 36-

hour drive from the U.S.-Mexico border. Sometimes Juan Alvarez goes alone; sometimes he takes one of the boys.

"Each trip takes three or four days, and we go about ten times a year. We go wherever the pastor tells us to go," says Marc, "to deliver the food and clothes, and for my father to go to their churches and preach."

• • •

"I WORRY. I WORRY about who the boys will follow," says Juan Alvarez, talking about the forces he fears in his own neighborhood. "I call them street fighters. These kids who survive on the street. They're never home. Their father don't care, their mother don't care. I worry my sons will follow these kids."

Alvarez explains that keeping his children clear of negative influences has always been a concern. "We have problems in this neighborhood," says Juan, gesturing down his street. "One lady, she drinks like a horse," he continues, adding that in the afternoons, the woman sits on the front step with music blaring from inside her house.

"All the kids from the neighborhood go play by the bridge," a shallow conduit on the other side of the Alvarez house, across a vacant lot. Alvarez explains it's often the scene for confrontations between neighborhood boys. "Maybe I'm wrong, but I don't teach my boys to fight back," says Juan. "I tell them, if there's bad language, don't answer in the same words. I see the anger, and words lead to fists, then knives and guns."

"The other day, this little boy from the neighborhood went home, and told his mother one of our boys hit him. So, she didn't come to us. She sent the big brother, and he punched Marc in the eye." Indeed, Marc has a discolored area around one eye. "Then the police came, and [the mother] wants them to come after Marc," says Alvarez, shaking his head. Rosa Alvarez speaks to her husband in Spanish.

"We just have to live our life," concludes Juan, "and she lives hers."

• • •

In the fall of 1995, Juan and Rosa moved their sons to Faith Outreach, while Myra advanced to ninth grade at New Life Christian Academy. The cost for each child was $2,500, payable in $250-per-month increments across a ten-month schedule. San Antonio CEO provided $70 per month for each child; Juan's share was $180 times three, for a total of $540. Juan got a $100 per month discount by helping the pastor at Faith Outreach, and volunteering to go on church missions to Mexico. With no other income than his Social Security disability payments, Juan and Rosa Alvarez took on a $4,400 a year tuition commitment.

Money is an inescapable issue for the Alvarez family. Myra Alvarez, showing disapproval befitting an elder sibling, says: "Sometimes it's frustrating. My brothers don't see how much everything costs, and what my parents do for them."

"The boys see something they want," says Juan Alvarez, "I say, we all want. Mom needs new glasses, but we don't have the money, so she don't get them right now. I tell them, look in the driveway. I have a '74 truck; I would like a 1999. We do without these things."

"And then if they keep telling me, get me this, I say, get me good grades, and we'll see."

• • •

JUAN ALVAREZ TELLS ME about the moment when he began to realize how his children's new schools had begun to change them. A few weeks after Myra had started high school at New Life, Juan and his daughter were at the shopping mall when Myra saw some friends from her old school. Her father waited—"I stood far away," says Juan, smiling, "you know, how you have to when they are that age"—while Myra talked with her friends for a few minutes. On the way home Myra said to her father, "Did you see them, Dad? Their makeup is so ugly, and they look so angry, so tough." Juan was silent. Myra asked him why. He said: "Because last year, that was you."

Looking back, Myra Alvarez says she no longer keeps up with the kids from Horace Mann. "I had my little ghetto friends, with those baggy jeans my dad hated," she says, laughing, "but I don't really associate with anyone from the neighborhood anymore."

"It's different now. They don't want to move up in life. They're either pregnant, or living with somebody, or married, not that it's bad to be married," says Myra, "but I think nineteen is a little young."

"Me, I want to get my associate's [degree], and then go to UTSA [University of Texas at San Antonio] for a business degree. And I want to travel. I haven't really been anywhere. I want to work in business," continues Myra. "Maybe with a big company, where I can do some travel."

I ask Myra to think back to the time she made the switch from Horace Mann to private school. "Everything's changed. I have a totally different perspective. In terms of school, and what we learned," says Myra, "and morally, also. Like I said about the girls we used to go to school with, being pregnant and all. Even my job: if I hadn't gone to private school, I never would have heard about working at Kelly," the Air Force base just south of the Alvarez home.

"I played soccer at public school, but I got into track in private school," says Myra. "As a freshman, I started in sprints, but by tenth grade, I was running the two-mile. That was my year. I won three medals at States in track, and one in cross country."

"It was track, school, and work. We used to get up at 5 o'clock to run," says Myra of the training regimen she and her teammates followed. "We'd run along Highway 90, and then past the edge of Kelly Air Force Base. They would be training the new recruits real early, too," recalls Myra, laughing. "We'd hear gunshots from the rifle range. It made us run a little faster."

In June 1999, Myra Alvarez graduated from New Life Christian Academy. Today, Myra works full time at Kelly as a clerical support clerk. Recently, she won her third promotion, "I'm a GS-3 now," she says, "my third grade increase in three years."

She also attends Saint Philips community college part-time at night. "I'm doing my basic requirements for a business major." Myra worked at Kelly part-time through high school, earning enough to pay for her books, her school uniform and her lunches at New Life, Juan Alvarez is careful to note, proud of his daughter's investment in her own education. For her last two years at New Life, Myra contributed $50 a month from her Kelly paycheck to her own tuition. "And she still had time to be a runner," says her father.

Rosa Alvarez, who has left the room while her husband was speaking, returns with a canvas tote bag. She zips it open to reveal the tangle of ribbons and medals Myra brought home from track meets across Texas and beyond.

• • •

IT HAS BEEN FIVE YEARS since Juan Alvarez wrote his letter to San Antonio CEO. Since then, he has become more aware of the struggle to expand educational alternatives—and on occasion, involved in the struggle itself.

In the summer of 1995, Juan joined several dozen other San Antonio CEO parents on a bus ride to Austin, where the Texas legislature was embroiled in a voucher battle.

They went simply to show support, with the idea that they might be able to meet with a legislator or two to convey their own experiences as part of the CEO program. At around 2 A.M., Teresa Treat, the executive director of San Antonio CEO, asked Alvarez if he would be willing to testify. Juan hadn't expected that, and had prepared nothing. He was nervous: "Talking with legislators, lawyers, professors and teachers, it was something I didn't think of before." Still, he agreed.

"I told them what it was like for me, as a parent," recalls Juan. "I talked to them from the heart. I told them I was there not for my own children only, but for all children. They all need education, opportunity."

"I don't know how long I talked or just how I said what I said. But just before I was going to stop, a story came to me. I can't remember where it is I heard it from. A story of this lady, an old, old, old lady. She is in her garden, planting a peach tree. Her grandson comes along and sees his grandmother working. 'What you doing?' he says. He knows his grandmother won't ever live long enough to get the peaches from that tree."

"And the old lady says, 'When you have your sons, when they go to asking who planted this tree, you will tell them about me.'"

"So I said to the legislators," Alvarez recalls, "this is how it is."

"Probably, you won't see the fruit right now. I won't see the fruit. But the seed is planted. There will be fruit."

Juan stopped. There was silence in the hearing room, then applause. "I see some of them. They are blinking," recalls Alvarez, "trying not to cry." State Representative Paul Sadler, the Democrat representative of District 8, took Alvarez aside. "He told me, 'You don't know how far this thing will go. You are doing so much. You are an example for all of us.'"

• • •

TWIN BROTHERS MARC AND MARIANO Alvarez enter the living room, and take up positions at opposite ends of a gold brocade couch. Seventh graders now, each slumps against an armrest, their tennis shoes nearly touching on the carpeted floor. Behind them, the wall serves as a family photo gallery, with pictures of Juan, Rosa, and the children at various ages.

"My boys," says Juan, "they're open in their opinions. They don't shrink back like kids. What they think, they say straight out."

And indeed, the boys are candid as I ask them about their experiences at school and growing up in West San Antonio.

Until recently, the Alvarez boys attended the same schools, moving from Nelson Elementary to Faith Outreach, and when Faith Outreach closed, to another private school called Lakeview Christian. Now, for the first time, they will be separated. While Marc stayed at Lakeview, Mariano has transferred to another church-run school, the School of Leadership.

"They were pulling each other down," says Alvarez, as the boys sit impassively, listening to their father. "We thought it is time to move them apart." I learn that Juan had a little help coming to that conclusion, when Mariano got suspended from Lakeview Christian.

"I was fooling around," says Mariano, "and I sprayed a kid with air freshener. They kicked me out." With Mariano suspended, Juan and Rosa Alvarez began the search to find their son a new school.

"I wasted almost three weeks," says Mariano, "I had to stay home, do whatever work my father and mother told me. Fixing things up, clearing out garbage, working on the cars. Or just sitting there, doing nothing, if they told me to."

"When that's it every day, I mean, each minute is so long," Mariano continues. "I was glad to get back in school. I told my father not to worry. I won't do anything stupid like that again."

Both boys are average students, earning mostly C's. They're active in sports, favoring cross-country and track. "I tell them, all the time, go to college. Study. But sports," says Juan, "that's good, too. The boys like running on the track team, like their sister. They play basketball. And Mariano, he likes soccer."

"I want to go to Texas Tech, over on San Pedro," says Marc Alvarez, referring to the university just a few blocks from the Alvarez home. I ask him whether he's ever thought about going to college outside San Antonio. "No. I don't want to go far. I'd miss my family."

"I want to study to be a scientist. Working on DNA, on AIDs and things like that," says Marc, "something to help people."

Mariano talks about college too, but has a different goal: "I want to be a track star. I want to go to Texas A&M, and be on the track team there. I do 300-meter hurdles, the 110 hurdles."

When asked the differences they see between public and private schools, the boys speak as one.

"Private schools are different," says Marc Alvarez. "In sixth grade, you're already learning Algebra I. In public school, it's still addition and subtraction. They're three or four years behind, just in what they ask you to do. I see kids who still can't read, moving up [a grade]. I don't see that's fair."

Mariano steps in. "The teachers have a love of learning. A feeling for the children. You can see it."

"In the public school, it's like teachers' hands are tied," says Marc. "I don't know why. It just is."

• • •

"I SEE MY PARENTS SACRIFICE, give up a lot. That's one reason I want to start working after school," says Mariano, whose parents, for now at least, oppose the idea. "I could work at McDonald's, and start paying back my parents for all the money they've spent for my school."

Mariano mentions the Horizon program, which, in contrast to San Antonio CEO, provides full tuition grants to families in the Edgewood school district, which ends at the corner of Northwest 27th Street and Culebra, about one mile southwest of the Alvarez's home.

Mariano asks: "We can't get in that, can we?" Even the Alvarez children seem aware of the way an accident of geography has put them just beyond reach of a program that would cover their entire private school tuition, with the financial relief that would provide their parents.

Juan Alvarez seems to see this as a chance to impress upon his sons that such unfairness is the way of the world. "Some get it all paid. Some get some paid. And some get nothing."

"It's like I say: We are the pioneers," says Alvarez, glancing at his sons on the couch. "We fight the war, even if we don't get the benefit. And one day, we win."

Policy Postscript

Does Choice Work?

DOES SCHOOL CHOICE WORK? Milwaukee, Cleveland, and a wide array of philanthropically financed choice programs are generating considerable data with which to judge the impact of voucher programs. Eight different studies of five different choice programs conducted by four different research teams—ranging from assessments led by University of Wisconsin's John F. Witte and Princeton's Cecelia Rouse to Harvard's Paul Peterson and Indiana University's Kim Metcalf—have produced what Manhattan Institute researcher Jay Greene calls a "remarkable amount of consensus"[14] on the positive impact of school choice.

In the world of public policy research, the five programs in question (Milwaukee's Parental Choice, Cleveland's Scholarship Program, plus privately funded choice programs in New York City, Dayton, Ohio, and Washington, D.C.) offer an unusual opportunity to assess the impact of choice through controlled experiments. Because all five programs award vouchers through a random, lottery-style system, they allow researchers to compare school choice students to ready-made control groups comprised of students who

---

[14] Jay Greene, "A Survey of Results from Voucher Experiments: Where We Are and What We Know," Harvard Program on Education Policy and Governance, March 2000, p. 4.

remain in public school, differing only by virtue of having "lost" the voucher lottery.

These unique research conditions provide evidence of the emerging consensus on several questions that bear directly on whether choice works:

- What do parents think about choice programs?
- Do choice students' test scores show improvement?
- What is the impact of choice on school segregation?
- And finally, is *private* school choice a catalyst for *public* school change?

PARENTAL SATISFACTION

AS RESEARCHER JAY GREENE observes, in terms of parental satisfaction, "the evidence in support of school choice is unambiguous and overwhelmingly positive."[15] In every study in every city, parents display strong positive attitudes on the value of choice schools for their children.

In Cleveland, two sets of evaluators came to similar conclusions on parental satisfaction. As the head of the Indiana University research team put it:

> Parents of scholarship students tend to be much more satisfied with their child's school than other parents... [S]cholarship recipient parents are more satisfied with the child's teachers, more satisfied with the academic standards at the child's school, more satisfied with order and discipline, [and] more satisfied with social activities at the school.[16]

The Indiana University findings are seconded by a separate set of Cleveland studies. Paul Peterson's team reports that almost 50 percent of choice parents were "very satisfied" with their choice school's academics, safety and disciplinary environment, and overall moral values, compared with a 30 percent "satisfaction rate" on the part of Cleveland public school parents.[17] The

---

[15.] Jay Greene, "A Survey of Results from Voucher Experiments: Where We Are and What We Know," Harvard Program on Education Policy and Governance, March 2000, p. 5.

[16.] Kim K. Metcalf, "Evaluation of the Cleveland Scholarship and Tutoring Program, 1996-1999," unpublished manuscript, Indiana University, 1999, p. 20.

same satisfaction rates prevail in San Antonio, both in the Horizon program, where 61 percent of choice parents are satisfied with the academic quality of their children's schools, compared with 35 percent of public school parents,[18] and in San Antonio CEO, where the percentage of parents "very satisfied" with the "amount children learned" rose from 19 percent at the student's previous public school to 60 percent at the choice school, while the percentage of parents "very satisfied" with school discipline rose from 12 percent at the child's previous public school to 56 percent at the choice school.[19]

What of Milwaukee, the primary target of voucher opponents? From the very beginning, the reports of official evaluator John F. Witte consistently found high levels of parental satisfaction:

> Parents... believe they found in the choice schools what they professed they were looking for when they entered the program—increased learning and discipline.[20]

SCORE WARS

AS AN EARLY INDICATOR, parental satisfaction may be a sign of a well-designed choice program; yet no amount of parental satisfaction will substitute for a program's impact on student educational achievement.

As ground zero in the voucher wars, Milwaukee has had the longest experience with private school choice, offering evaluators the earliest opportunity

---

[17.] Paul E. Peterson, William G. Howell, and Jay P. Greene, "An Evaluation of the Cleveland Voucher Program After Two Years," Harvard Program on Education Policy and Governance Working Paper, 1998.

[18.] Paul E. Peterson, David Myers, and William G. Howell, "An Evaluation of the Horizon Scholarship Program in the Edgewood Independent School District, San Antonio, Texas: The First Year," Harvard Program on Education Policy and Governance Working Paper, September 1999, p. 3.

[19.] Kenneth Godwin, Frank Kemerer, Valerie Martinez, Carrie Ausbrooks and Kay Thomas, "An Evaluation of the San Antonio CEO Private Scholarship Program," University of North Texas, 1996, p. 3, Table 2.

[20.] John F. Witte, Christopher A Thorn, Kim M. Pritchard, and Michele Claibourn, "Fourth Year Report, Milwaukee Parental Choice Program," University of Wisconsin-Madison, December 1994, p. 20.

to observe the effect of choice on student achievement. For the first five years of the Milwaukee program, annual assessments were done by John F. Witte, the University of Wisconsin academic hand-picked as official examiner by then-state superintendent Herbert Grover, a sworn enemy of the voucher program. Witte's annual assessments reported "no substantial difference over the life of the program between the Choice and MPS students, especially the low-income MPS students."[21] Not surprisingly, Witte's work quickly became the weapon of first resort in the hands of anti-voucher forces, as critics selectively culled the reports for ammunition against school choice.[22]

Pressured by other researchers to allow access to the Milwaukee data, Witte relented in early 1996, releasing his data onto the World Wide Web. Contrary to Witte's findings, new studies reported significant gains by Milwaukee's choice students. Economist Cecilia Rouse of Princeton identified "quite large," statistically significant gains in choice students' math scores: gains of 1.5 to 2.3 Normal Curve Equivalent (NCE)[23] points per year.[24]

A second reassessment of the Milwaukee data by Paul Peterson and Jay Greene raised questions about Witte's studies,[25] after finding that students in the Choice program for three or four years registered reading scores 3 to 5

---

[21] John F. Witte, "The Milwaukee Voucher Experiment," *Educational Evaluation and Policy Analysis*, Vol. 20, No. 4, Winter, 1999, pp. 236–7.

[22] In fact, Witte was never as unrelievedly critical of the Milwaukee program as voucher critics made him out to be; witness Witte's endorsement of programs such as the Milwaukee Parental Choice Program in a book published earlier this year:

"Choice can be a useful tool to aid families and educators in inner city and poor communities where education has been a struggle for several generations. If programs are devised correctly, they can provide meaningful educational choices to families that now do not have such choices. And it is not trivial that most people in America, and surely most reading this book, already have those choices." (John F. Witte, *The Market Approach to Education*, Princeton University Press, 2000, p. 6)

For a more detailed assessment of the early Milwaukee evaluations, see Chapters 10 and 11, "Report Card: Accentuate the Negative… Eliminate the Positive," in Daniel McGroarty, *Break These Chains; the Battle for School Choice*, Prima Publishing (1996).

[23] NCE is the commonly used comparison metric by which scores on various tests are converted to score equivalents on the Iowa Test of Basic Skills.

[24] Cecilia Rouse, "Private School Vouchers and Student Achievement: An Evaluation of the Milwaukee Parental Choice Program," *The Quarterly Journal of Economics*, volume CXIII, issue 2, May 1998, p. 593.

percentile points higher than their public school peers, while math scores out-paced public school students by 5 to 12 percentile points.[26]

[25.] Greene and Peterson raised questions about "inaccurate test score data" utilized by Witte in "Effectiveness of School Choice: The Milwaukee Experiment," Harvard Program on Education Policy and Governance, March 1997, p. 26:

"Subsequent to issuing Greene et al., 1996, we discovered that the Milwaukee test score data available on theWorldWide Web do not adjust for the fact that some students are not promoted from one grade to the next. For example, students in both test and control groups who were held back for a year at the end of the third grade were scored as third graders when they otherwise would have been scored as fourth graders. When this happens, a student can receive a much higher percentile score than is appropriate. Other students are allowed to skip a grade, and if this promotion is not taken into account, it produces an error of the opposite kind. We were able to eliminate both types of error by adjusting test scores to the correct grade level...."

In a response to Witte's criticism of their re-evaluation, Greene and Peterson catalogue the problems with Witte's methodological approach in "Methodological Issues in Evaluation Research: The Milwaukee School Choice Plan," Harvard Program on Education Policy and Governance, August 1996, p. 2:

"Witte's response... does not deny that the Witte research team compared low-income, minority choice students to a more advantaged cross-section of Milwaukee public school students. It does not justify the assumptions the Witte team had to make in order to estimate school effects by means of linear regression on this particular data set. It does not deny that the response rate for the data used in Witte's main regression analyses relied upon a data set that had more than 80 percent of its cases missing and in which the evidence that the missing cases contaminated the evidence is very strong. It does not deny that many of the regressions he used employ a measure of family income—student participation in the subsidized school lunch program—that other data in the evaluation reveal to be a very poor proxy for family income."

[26.] Jay Greene and Paul Peterson, "The Effectiveness of School Choice in Milwaukee: A Secondary Analysis of Data from the Program's Evaluation," presented at the August 1996 American Political Science Association annual conference, p. 4.

Jay Greene adds a caveat to the Milwaukee findings, noting: "Unfortunately the confidence that we can have in these findings is limited by the amount of missing data caused by high student mobility among poor families and incomplete data collection. The findings after three or four years in the program are based on test scores from 40 percent of the choice students and 48 percent of the control group students. There is, however, good reason to believe that the students' missing test scores did not differ systematically from those for whom we had data. After three or four years our treatment and control groups did not differ significantly from each other in background characteristics collected when they applied, suggesting that little bias was introduced by missing data. They did not significantly differ on their math or reading test scores, their family income, their mother's education, their rate of single parenthood, or the amount of time parents spent with children. We also conducted an "intention to treat" analysis to test for the possibility that selective attrition from the program biased results.... The results...were basically the same as the main analysis, 11 NCE point gain in math and 6 NCE point gain in reading."

In the supercharged atmosphere surrounding choice score wars, former Milwaukee Public School Superintendent Howard L. Fuller observed the irony in voucher opponents' efforts to downplay and discredit the Milwaukee findings:

> ...if the preliminary results [from the Milwaukee Parental Choice Program]...were to have occurred in *public school* experiments, those now seeking to halt them instead would be pushing for a rapid expansion.[27]

If the post-Witte reassessment of Milwaukee Parental Choice suggests significant achievement gains for choice students over time, what about Cleveland and San Antonio?

Two years into San Antonio's Horizon experiment, no data on student achievement scores have been reported. As a philanthropically funded private school choice program, San Antonio CEO has been less studied than the legislatively enacted programs in Milwaukee or Cleveland; even so, a 1995 assessment found that students who had transferred out of public school on a CEO voucher averaged 8.14 NCE points higher in reading and 9.91 points higher in math achievement, after one year in their choice school. [28]

In Cleveland, results from the two research teams studying the choice program differ in degree, but point to a positive impact on student achievement. Kim Metcalf of the Indiana University team reports:

> ...Results indicate that scholarship students in existing private schools had significantly higher test scores than public school students in language (45.0 versus 40.0) and science (40.0 versus 36.0). However, there were no statistically sig-

---

[27.] Howard L. Fuller, "A Research Update on School Choice," *Current Education Issues*: No. 97-3, November 1997, p. 16, emphasis added.

[28.] Valerie Martinez, Kenneth Godwin and Frank Kemerer, "Comparing Private and Public School Choice in San Antonio," University of North Texas, January 1995, p. 7. NCE conversion was used to allow comparisons between the Iowa Test of Basic Skills and other tests administered by participating private schools.

The San Antonio researchers add this caveat: "Because we do not have a group of private choosing parents who did not get their choice, we cannot say that the positive impact is due to the private school. Some portion of this effect is due to coming from a choosing family."

nificant differences between these groups on any of the other scores.[29]

With test scores from only two choice schools, Greene, Peterson, and Howell's Cleveland study has limitations as well. Even so, the findings are noteworthy:

> We found that after two years students at the two schools we examined had gains of 7.5 national percentile points (NPR) in reading and 15.6 NPR in math. These gains were achieved despite the fact that the students at these two schools were among the most disadvantaged students in Cleveland.[30]

These reported gains stand in sharp contrast to the common experience in public schools, where achievement scores of the average inner city public school student actually *decline* 1 to 2 points each year he or she is in school.[31]

Even with these impressive gains, choice students in Cleveland and Milwaukee[32] average around the 40th percentile on achievement tests.[33] However, given the base from which they begin, if choice students continue to make progress year after year, it will mark an extraordinary breakthrough in lifting the achievement of low-income children.

[29.] Metcalf, "Evaluation of the Cleveland Scholarship and Tutoring Program," p. 15.

[30.] Paul E. Peterson, William G. Howell, and Jay P. Greene, "An Evaluation of the Cleveland Voucher Program After Two Years," Harvard Program on Education Policy and Governance, 1998, Table 12.

[31.] See, for example, Jay Greene, William Howell and Paul Peterson in "Lessons from the Cleveland Scholarship Program," in *Learning from School Choice* (Brookings Institution, 1998), p. 382:
"According to the office overseeing desegregation in Cleveland, Cleveland public school reading scores declined, on average, by 1 to 2 percentile points between both the first and second grades and between the second and third grades in the years 1994–5 to 1995–6. …[O]ther researchers have found a similar pattern in the Milwaukee choice experiment."

[32.] The lack of multi-year test scores for San Antonio choice students make it impossible to assess their ongoing achievement.

[33.] See Greene and Peterson, "Effectiveness of School Choice: The Milwaukee Experiment," Harvard Program on Education Policy and Governance, March 1997, Table 2. For Cleveland data, see Peterson, Howell, and Greene, "An Evaluation of the Cleveland Voucher Program After Two Years," Harvard Program on Education Policy and Governance, Table 12.

Indeed, evidence that vouchers raise student achievement continues to mount. In August 2000, a joint Harvard, Georgetown University, and University of Wisconsin study of privately funded voucher programs in Washington, D.C., New York City and Dayton, Ohio—three of the cities where lottery-style selection policies create a natural control group—showed that, over a two year period, black students moving to private schools via vouchers scored a significant *six percentile points higher* than their peers who stayed behind in public school. As one of the study's authors noted, gains that great close the national test-score gap between black and white students by one-third.[34]

CHOOSING BY RACE?

VOUCHER OPPONENTS quite often accompany their claims that choice has no positive educational impact for students with charges that it will have significant and negative social impact in terms of re-segregating America's schools. As the ACLU's Nadine Strossen puts it:

> The fact that private schools may discriminate on the basis of income, coupled with the racially based income disparities in our society, means that vouchers likely would cause public schools to become even more racially segregated.[35]

Or as UCLA's Amy Stuart Wells posits:

> ...competition between schools for students will not lead to overall educational improvement but will quite possibly lead to greater racial and social-class segregation and stratification.[36]

[34.] The voucher effect was largest in the District of Columbia, where students scored 9 percentile points better than their public school counterparts. William G. Howell, Patrick J. Wolf, Paul E. Peterson and David E. Campbell, "Test-Score Effects of School Vouchers in Dayton, Ohio, New York City, and Washington, D.C.: Evidence from Randomized Field Trials," Harvard Program on Education Policy and Governance, August 2000. See also "Study Shows Vouchers Boost Test Scores for Blacks," *The Washington Post*, August 28, 2000.

[35.] Nadine Strossen, False Choices, *Intellectualcapital.com*, December 3, 1998.

David Berliner, Dean of Education at Arizona State University, goes even further:

> Voucher programs would allow for splintering along racial and ethnic lines...[V]oucher programs could end up resembling the ethnic cleansing occurring in Kosovo.[37]

Since these hypothetical horrors are predictions of what might happen if vouchers were available to families of all income levels, the experience of voucher programs designed solely for low-income families cannot dispel all the scare stories. Yet the experience of these targeted programs points in a surprising direction: choice leads to more integration, not less.

Data from San Antonio, where the Horizon experiment involves a very homogeneous ethnic population in a district about one-eighth the size of Milwaukee, is inconclusive; the mix of students using vouchers closely mirrors the public school district's overall ethnic profile, which in both cases is over 90 percent Hispanic. In Cleveland, however, Jay Greene has found:

> Nearly a fifth of the participants in [the Cleveland choice program] attend private schools that have a racial composition that resembles the average racial composition of the Cleveland area. Only 5.2 percent of public school students attend similarly integrated schools.
>
> The evidence from Cleveland's school choice program shows that children are more likely to attend a racially integrated school if their families are allowed to choose a private school than if they remain in public schools.... Critics will no longer be able to argue that school choice promotes divisiveness and segregation.[38]

---

36. Amy Stuart Wells, "The Sociology of School Choice," in *School Choice: Examining the Evidence*, Edith Rasell and Richard Rothstein, eds., Economic Policy Institute, 1993, p. 30.

37. "Arizona Dean Warns of Possible Ethnic Splits," *The Albuquerque Journal*, May 8, 1999.

38. "Choice and Community: The Racial, Economic, and Religious Context of Parental Choice in Cleveland," Jay P. Greene, Harvard Program on Education Policy and Governance, November 1999. The report is available on-line at *www.buckeyeinstitute.org*.

In short, Greene summarizes: "Choice appears conducive to integration, while government assignment to public school appears conducive to segregation."

Emerging data from Milwaukee suggests that Cleveland's experience is no aberration. Howard L. Fuller and George Mitchell have found "nearly twice as many Milwaukee Public School elementary students...in racially isolated schools"[39] compared with Milwaukee's Catholic elementary schools, which welcomed a wave of choice students when the Wisconsin Supreme Court upheld the constitutionality of Milwaukee Parental Choice in 1998. According to *Investor's Business Daily*, Fuller's and Mitchell's studies suggest that "...vouchers are serving as a catalyst for racial harmony in Milwaukee schools once beyond the reach of minority parents."[40]

CHOICE AS CATALYST

IN ADDITION TO ADVANCING the equity argument that credits choice with expanding poor parents' educational options, pro-voucher advocates frequently claim that choice will act as a catalyst for *public* school change.

This has not yet happened in Cleveland, where the public school graduation rate is 32 percent[41] and the city's public schools recently received a score

[39]. Defined as schools having more than 90 percent or fewer than 10 percent minority enrollment. See pp. 5–6, Howard L. Fuller and George A. Mitchell, "The Impact of School Choice on Racial and Ethnic Enrollment in Milwaukee Private Schools," *Current Education Issues*, No. 99–5, December 1999, pp. 5–6. Fuller and Mitchell revisited the issue in a July 2000 study, which found that after a quarter century of desegregation efforts "50 percent of Milwaukee Public School students attend racially isolated schools," while "only 30.1 percent of students at religious schools that use vouchers fall into that category." See "Vouchers Promote Diversity," *Investor's Business Daily*, July 6, 2000.

[40]. "Vouchers Promote Diversity," *Investor's Business Daily*, July 6, 2000.

Indeed, even John F. Witte's official evaluations also found that the choice program fosters diversity, an ideal otherwise dear to the public education establishment, but inconvenient when it comes as a consequence of school vouchers. As early as 1993, Witte wrote: "The student bodies of participating [choice] schools vary from schools that are almost all one minority race, to racially integrated schools, to schools that have used the program to diversify their almost all White student bodies." (John F. Witte, "Third Year Report, Milwaukee Parental Choice Program," University of Wisconsin-Madison, December 1993, pp. v and 18)

of zero out of 27 on the state's education report card. There is no evidence that the public system has chosen reform as a means to compete with the Cleveland voucher program. Indeed, it appears far more likely that the public education establishment has pinned its hopes on prevailing in court to kill the Cleveland Scholarship Program, and returning to the educational *status quo ante.*

In San Antonio, the Edgewood public school district saw the Horizon voucher program as reason to mount a public relations push rather than a reform effort. As Edgewood Superintendent Dolores Muñoz put it: "We're launching a strategic marketing plan to sell ourselves and keep the community informed."[42]

If Edgewood has been reluctant to consider changes in the classroom as a means to combat the appeal of vouchers, it has moved quickly to address the budgetary implications of the Horizon alternative. Breaking a long-standing "gentleman's agreement" not to poach students from neighboring public school districts, Edgewood has opened its doors to transfers from other public school districts, a move that will help the system recoup some of the financial losses caused by the exodus of voucher students. As for competing head to head to see how public school students might fare compared with voucher students, the Edgewood School Board voted not to cooperate in an outside evaluation measuring, among other things, the academic achievement of Horizon voucher students versus their public school peers.[43] Indeed, as Horizon's Robert Aguirre recounts, such is the system's hostility toward Horizon that Edgewood suspended one public school teacher for helping children obtain applications for the voucher program.

What about Milwaukee, where that city's Parental Choice Program is now in its tenth year, and has survived court challenges in both state and federal court? Jay Greene notes that "the [Milwaukee] public schools have promised

---

[41.] See Cleveland Scholarship Program appellants' brief (*Simmons-Harris, et al., v. Zelman, et al.,* March 31, 2000), p. 20.

[42.] "A Leader in the Storm," *San Antonio Express,* January 1, 1998.

[43.] CEO America press release on the Edgewood-Horizon Project, February 9, 1999.

to provide individual tutoring to any student not reading at grade level by Grade 3, a policy that they have advertised on billboards."[44]

A recent *Dallas Morning News* article provides a snapshot of the Milwaukee Public School system's reaction to private school choice. A teacher at Benjamin Franklin Elementary, a Milwaukee grade school, complains about the number of students using vouchers to leave her school, adding that "schools have to advertise now to get kids to our public schools. We shouldn't have to. This is absurd." Even so, the article goes on to note that, five years ago, Benjamin Franklin "was ranked third from the bottom among Milwaukee public elementary schools because of low test scores." A new principal took the helm, instituting

> new programs, including the heavy use of phonics exercises in the early grades, after consulting with a team of educators. The school today is ranked about average, compared with the rest of the district.[45]

The Benjamin Franklin experience appears to be emblematic of more systemic change. Howard L. Fuller, who served for four years as superintendent of the Milwaukee Public Schools and is now a strong supporter of school choice, identifies seven ways that Milwaukee's public schools have changed for the better as a result of the competition from private school vouchers. Parental Choice, Fuller says, has resulted in the Milwaukee Public Schools:

- Opening new charter schools—from a single charter school in 1995, the year the Wisconsin legislature voted to open the Milwaukee voucher program to religious schools, to seven charter schools for the 2000–2001 school year.

- Expanding early childhood education options—including full-day 5-year-old kindergarten, as well as an expansion of 80 percent of MPS's 4–

---

[44] Jay P. Greene, "A Survey of Results from Voucher Experiments: Where We Are and What We Know," Harvard Program on Education Policy and Governance, March 2000, p. 16.

[45] "A Study on Vouchers; Milwaukee School System is at the Center of Debate," *Dallas Morning News*, July 10, 2000.

K programs to all-day programs, and a tripling of the number of 3–K programs.

- Expanding before- and after-school programs for low-income students— from a single program in 1995 to 82 programs at present, serving 28,000 children.
- Expanding school-based student health clinics—from two in 1995 to 47 today.
- Expanding MPS's "specialty" schools—the city's popular and always over-subscribed magnet school program, which with expansion has seen waiting lists shrink in recent years by 40 percent.
- Supporting increased accountability, as the Milwaukee School Board repelled efforts to water down the detailed school report cards instituted by Superintendent Fuller.
- Strengthening graduation requirements, with the Milwaukee School Board prevailing against spirited resistance from the school system.

Fuller goes on to note that in the past year alone, Milwaukee's public school authorities have permitted a dozen schools to hire teachers outside the seniority system, and acceded to longstanding requests by parents for more schools offering popular programs such as Montessori instruction.[46] According to Fuller, "Taken together, [these reforms] represent a real effort to make MPS more responsive and accountable to parents of Milwaukee children. Such a change is an essential pre-requisite to educational reform."[47]

• • •

UNDERNEATH THE RHETORICAL SALVOS, the actual experience of choice, though still tentative and based on a handful of small, city-specific programs, allays some of voucher critics' worst fears, while fulfilling some of voucher advocates' best hopes. In the sterile surroundings of a science lab,

[46.] With most of the Milwaukee Public School changes commencing with the 1998–99 school year, it remains to be seen whether the new initiatives will translate into improved achievement scores for MPS students.

[47.] *Howard L. Fuller affidavit, Ruth D. Holmes, et al., v. John Ellis "Jeb" Bush, et al.,* Florida First District Court of Appeals, Case 99-3370, April 2000.

that might signal the end of conflict, and the emergence of consensus. The choice debate, however, is more street fight than science experiment. One empirical question, it seems, will always be unanswered: Can any amount of evidence overcome an implacable antipathy to school choice?

Is Choice Constitutional?

IS SCHOOL CHOICE CONSTITUTIONAL? Voucher opponents answer with a categorical no. "Pro-voucher forces are on a collision course with state constitutions and with the Establishment Clause of the First Amendment," declares Carole Shields, president of People for the American Way, an organization that has been party to anti-voucher suits in Wisconsin, Ohio, Florida and other states.[48] For ACLU President Nadine Strossen, the case is closed: "...vouchers force all taxpayers to finance sectarian institutions, which violates the First Amendment's religious-liberty guarantee."

Somewhat surprisingly in the face of these claims, the constitutionality of using vouchers at religious schools has never been squarely addressed by the Supreme Court. In fact, when presented an opportunity to review the expanded Milwaukee Parental Choice Program, given a clean bill of constitutional health by the Wisconsin Supreme Court in June 1998, the U.S. Supreme Court declined to hear the appeal, in spite of the arguments advanced by the ACLU, People for the American Way, and public teacher unions.

Since the Milwaukee Parental Choice case, the Supreme Court has declined to hear appeals in two other cases involving private school choice. The impact of the Court's inaction is a split decision, with an Arizona case favor-

---

[48.] "Bush's Signature on Florida Voucher Bill Paves Way for Constitutional Showdown," People for the American Way press release, June 21, 1999.

ing the pro-voucher position, and a Maine ruling buttressing the anti-voucher argument.

In *Bagley v. Town of Raymond*, a case involving some rural Maine communities' two-century old tradition of "tuitioning"—a practice whereby towns too small to operate their own school system pay to enroll local children in public or private schools in another town—the Maine Supreme Court upheld a 1980 law prohibiting the use of "tuitioning" money at religious schools. In the Arizona case, the Court declined in October 1999 to review a 1997 Arizona law permitting state residents to take a $500 annual tax credit for donations to a private school choice program, letting stand the Arizona Supreme Court's ruling that the tax credit was constitutional.

The U.S. Supreme Court's next encounter with school choice is likely to involve the Cleveland choice program. In the spring of 1999, the Ohio Supreme Court struck down the Cleveland program on procedural grounds, while giving it a clean bill of constitutional health on church-state issues. In the summer of 1999, after the Ohio legislature reenacted the Cleveland program, voucher opponents took their challenge to federal rather than state court. On December 20, 1999, U.S. District Court Judge Solomon Oliver ruled that the Cleveland choice program violated the First Amendment's establishment clause. The Cleveland case is currently on appeal to the U.S. Court of Appeals for the Sixth Circuit, with a decision expected in fall 2000. Whether the Sixth Circuit reverses Judge Oliver and restores the Cleveland choice program or upholds the lower court ruling, the case is destined for the U.S. Supreme Court, perhaps as early as the 2001 session.

DUELING PRECEDENTS

As THE CLEVELAND CASE MAKES its way through the judicial system, the Court will likely be considering two lines of precedent.

The first, emphasized by voucher opponents, is a long line of establishment-clause jurisprudence. Under the Supreme Court's 1971 *Lemon* ruling, any action by the government that affects religious organizations must pass a three-pronged test: 1) the action must serve a secular purpose; 2) its primary effect must neither advance nor inhibit religion; and 3) the government must avoid excessive entanglement with religion.[49] Under *Lemon*, for instance, even limited government oversight of a voucher program to ensure accountability—precisely the kind of legislative oversight pro-voucher legislatures were pushed to build into choice programs to answer anti-voucher critics— could be construed as constituting the kind of "excessive entanglement" that would invalidate a voucher program.[50]

For voucher opponents, the controlling case in the *Lemon* line is *Nyquist*,[51] the Court's 1973 ruling that struck down a New York state statute providing various forms of public aid to private schools, including tuition reimbursement assistance.

As People for the American Way put it in its press release celebrating federal Judge Oliver's December 1999 ruling against the Cleveland Choice program:

> Today's ruling is consistent with other federal court decisions against the use of public funds to pay for tuition in religious schools, following the U.S. Supreme Court's still-applicable 1973 ruling in *Committee for Public Education and Religious Liberty v. Nyquist*. The Ohio voucher program parallels the New York state private school tuition reimbursement program stuck down in *Nyquist*, and the Ohio case

---

[49.] *Lemon v. Kurtzman* (1971) 403 US 602.

[50.] The application of *Lemon* alone does not dictate that a voucher scheme would be held unconstitutional, though it clearly raises the bar. The Cleveland Choice program offers a case in point: Even as the Ohio Supreme Court overturned the Cleveland program on a procedural point, Ohio's justices were quite clear on the church-state issue—exonerating the program on *Lemon* grounds:
"We conclude that the school voucher program has a secular legislative purpose, does not have the primary effect of advancing religion, and does not excessively entangle government with religion." (Ohio Justice Paul Pfiefer, for the majority, May 27, 1999.)
In the same vein, the Institute for Justice's Clint Bolick argues that the Cleveland voucher plan passes the *Lemon* test as well, since its "primary effect is educational, not religious." (E-mail exchange with the author, July 18, 2000.)

[51.] *Committee for Public Education v. Nyquist* (1973) 413 US 756.

may be the best opportunity for the Supreme Court to revisit the issue of vouchers.[52]

CONSTITUTIONAL DAYLIGHT?

THE DIFFICULTY FOR VOUCHER OPPONENTS is the existence of an alternative line of rulings, which—while not overturning *Lemon*—carves out a constitutionally permissible route for government aid to reach religious institutions, plus a little-noticed footnote in the *Nyquist* ruling that may leave a loophole large enough to accommodate a carefully crafted voucher program.

Beginning with *Mueller v. Allen* in 1983, and running through *Witters v. Department of Services for the Blind* (1986)[53] and *Zobrest v. Catalina Foothills School District* (1993),[54] the Court has held that whatever aid might ultimately flow to religious institutions is, in the words of *Mueller*, "only… a result of numerous private choices of individual parents of school-age children."[55]

The difference between current voucher programs like the Milwaukee and Cleveland models and so-called "parochi-aid" plans of the *Nyquist* era, which limited aid to private schools only, is that today's voucher plans typically observe a *neutrality* toward all parental choices, public or private. Vouchers can be used at out-of-district public schools as well as private schools—and at private schools of any sort, religious or non-religious. In such instances, a voucher constitutes aid to *an individual*—the parent—not aid to *an institution*, the private school. As aid to individuals and not institutions, vouchers used for tuition at private religious schools do not breach the Establishment Clause

---

[52.] "Federal Court Overturns Ohio Vouchers," December 20, 1999.

[53.] In *Witters v. Department of Services for the Blind*, 474 US 481 (1986), the Supreme Court upheld the constitutionality of government-provided aid to a blind student studying for a divinity degree at a private Christian college.

[54.] *Zobrest v. Catalina Foothills School District* (1993) 113 S.Ct. 2462 allowed public aid to a deaf child enrolled in a religious school.

[55.] *Mueller v. Allen* (1983), 463 US at 398. In *Mueller*, the Court upheld a state law allowing educational expense income tax deductions for parents whose children attended private schools—despite the fact that most of the students attended religious schools.

because the government does not dictate or direct the destination of the funds.[56]

This same reasoning supports federal student loans, which students can use to enroll at the college of their choice, whether it's North Carolina or Notre Dame, Yeshiva or Yale. The same rationale also entitles low-income parents to federal child-care tax credits against the expense of enrolling their children not only in public day care facilities but in private, church-based child care centers if they so choose. At issue is whether these precedents for child-care and college grants, which bracket the K–12 education experience, point to the constitutionality of programs that provide public assistance to parents while maintaining a true neutrality between public, private, and religious schools.[57]

• • •

IT MAY BE TEMPTING TO CONCLUDE that *Lemon* and *Mueller* are simply parallel lines of precedent, each one open for the Court to choose, with no point of contact between them. Yet there is one point at which *Lemon* and *Mueller* cross paths, in a footnote in the *Nyquist* decision, that just might show present-day voucher advocates the way to constitutional daylight.

Even as the Court struck down the New York state statute in *Nyquist*, Justice Lewis Powell suggested:

> the significantly religious character of the statute's benefi-
> ciaries might differentiate the present case from a case
> involving....some form of public assistance (*e.g.*, scholar-
> ships) made available without regard to the sectarian-non-

[56.] *Zobrest* held that participating schools were "only incidental beneficiaries," aided only "as a result of the private decision of individual parents." (*Zobrest*, 113 S.Ct. at 2467)

Evidence is accumulating that the Supreme Court may indeed be carving out constitutionally permissible space for programs that provide indirect aid conditioned by private parental choices. In *Mitchell v. Helms*, a decision handed down June 28, 2000, the Court upheld by a 6-3 vote the public provision of computers and other materials for students at religious schools. Writing for the plurality, Justice Thomas noted the constitutionality of programs that maintain neutrality between public and private, religious schools, stating: "[N]othing in the establishment clause requires the exclusion of pervasively sectarian schools from otherwise permissible aid programs, and other doctrines of this court bar it. This doctrine, born of bigotry, should be buried now."

sectarian, or public-nonpublic nature of the institution benefited.[58]

In this reading, *Nyquist* leaves the door open to a certain species of voucher program very closely resembling the Milwaukee and Cleveland models.[59]

[57.] In addition to challenges in the federal courts, school choice faces constitutional challenges on the state level as well. In terms of litigation, the most important challenge comes in Florida, where Leon County Circuit Court Judge L. Ralph Smith ruled in March 2000 that the state's "opportunity scholarships"—a voucher program enacted in April 1999 as part of Governor Jeb Bush's "A+ Plan" school reform bill—violated the Florida state constitution. While both federal and state church-state issues were raised in the suit brought by Florida teachers unions, the ACLU, and the NAACP, Judge Smith directed the parties to brief only a narrower claim based on the Florida Constitution's Education Clause. In overturning the program, Judge Smith cited the Florida constitutional provision that obligates the state to provide all students with a "high quality education" through a "uniform, efficient, safe, secure, and high quality system of free public schools"—declining to rule on the church-state elements of the case. ("Private School Vouchers Found Unconstitutional in Florida," People for the American Way press release, March 14, 2000. See also PFAW, "In the Courts," at *www.pfaw.org*.) As this book was going to press, Florida's First District Court of Appeals voted 3-0 to reverse Judge Smith's ruling, giving a reprieve to Florida's voucher program. The case is now remanded to trial court for consideration of church-state issues. ("Florida Appeals Court Gives Voucher Movement a Victory," *The Wall Street Journal*, October 4, 2000)

State constitutional questions also come into play in a ballot initiative battle in Michigan, where voters will consider a November 2000 ballot measure to revise the state constitution to permit private school vouchers. The Michigan initiative would repeal a 1970 state constitutional amendment that banned public aid to religious schools, including indirect aid such as tax credits and deductions, a constraint that makes Michigan's constitution perhaps the most restrictive in the country on the issue of private school choice. Among other provisions, the Michigan ballot initiative would provide vouchers to all students currently attending failing school districts, defined as districts where the graduation rate is 67 percent or lower.

[58.] *Committee for Public Education v. Nyquist* (1971) 413 US at 738 n. 38.

[59.] Interestingly, the Wisconsin decision (*Jackson v. Benson* 97-0270) took notice of the anti-voucher *Nyquist* argument—and dismissed it:

"We reject the Respondents' argument that this case is controlled by *Committee for Pub. Educ. and Religious Liberty v. Nyquist*, 413 U.S. 756 (1973). Although the tuition reimbursement program in *Nyquist* closely parallels the amended MPCP, there are significant distinctions. In *Nyquist*, each of the facets of the challenged program directed aid exclusively to private schools and their students. The MPCP, by contrast, provides a neutral benefit to qualifying parents of school-age children in Milwaukee Public Schools. Unlike the program in *Nyquist*, the only financially-qualified Milwaukee students excluded from participation in the amended MPCP are those in the fourth grade or higher who are already attending private schools. The amended MPCP, viewed in its surrounding context, merely adds religious schools to a range of pre-existing educational choices available to MPS children. This seminal fact takes the amended MPCP out of the *Nyquist* construct and places it within the framework of *neutral education assistance programs*." Emphasis added.

According to Clint Bolick, vice president of the libertarian-leaning Institute for Justice and lead litigator for parents in the Milwaukee and Cleveland cases, the Cleveland program is, if anything, more constitutionally bullet-proof than the Milwaukee Parental Choice Program that has survived Supreme Court scrutiny. His reasoning hinges on the studied neutrality of the Cleveland program. First, says Bolick, "the Cleveland [plan] invites sub-urban public schools to participate," building private-public neutrality directly into the statute, whereas Milwaukee's Parental Choice simply assumes the existence of some degree of public school choice through the Milwaukee Public Schools' magnet or specialty schools. Second, as Bolick sees it, "Cleveland pays only 90 percent of private school tuition, assuring that there is no financial incentive to choose private schools," given that students who do transfer to a different public school can do so at no additional cost. In fact, Bolick notes, of all Cleveland students attending a school of their choice, 83 percent enroll at public magnet schools or community schools—Ohio's version of charter schools—while only 17 percent attend a private school via the Cleveland voucher program.[60]

"Those are major distinctions from *Nyquist*," Bolick concludes.

• • •

Which line of precedent will control the Cleveland voucher case? In the coming legal combat, pro-voucher forces enjoy support from an unlikely ally —liberal legal icon Laurence Tribe:

> These decisions [*Mueller* and *Witters*] suggest that the [Supreme] Court would uphold an educational voucher scheme that would permit parents to decide which schools, public or private, their children should attend. The Estab-lishment Clause probably would not stand as an obstacle to a purely neutral program, at least one with a broad enough class of beneficiary schools and one that channeled aid

[60.] Cleveland Scholarship Program, Appellants' brief, (*Simmons-Harris, et al., v. Zelman, et al.*, March 31, 2000), p. 22 and Table 2, page 23.

through parents and children rather than directly to schools.[61]

Tribe reiterated his position in 1991, after the passage of the original Milwaukee Parental Choice Program, adding by way of advice to voucher opponents:

> ...If there are objections [to vouchers], they should be debated on policy grounds, and not recast as constitutional arguments.[62]

[61.] Mark Bredemeier of the Landmark Legal Foundation should be credited for noting Tribe's stance, a staple in his arguments for the constitutionality of school choice. See Tribe's *American Constitutional Law*, 2nd Edition, Foundation Press, 1988, p. 1223.

[62.] "School 'Choice' a Tough Choice for Members of Congress," *The Congressional Quarterly*, April 27, 1991.

Who Chooses Choice?

WHO CHOOSES CHOICE? A seemingly innocuous question, but one with explosive potential for the voucher debate. After all, if already-advantaged children use vouchers, superior scores will prove nothing about the program's impact—and everything about the advantages choice students brought with them to their new private schools.

The argument that choice programs somehow attract or select "the cream of the crop" is a standard line of attack for choice opponents. As a rhetorical weapon, this claim packs a double-barrel charge, impugning the stated aims of choice programs, and at the same time inoculating public schools against the inevitable criticism, should choice students prove to outperform their public school peers.

Indeed, the argument is as old as the choice programs themselves. As the late Al Shanker, long-time head of the American Federation of Teachers, put it early in the Milwaukee Choice program's second year:

> If private schools can pick and choose the most promising students... what are the prospects for providing equal education opportunity to the children left behind?[63]

Other voucher opponents were quick to second Shanker's "cream of the crop" claim. Consider the Carnegie Foundation Report, issued to front page

---

[63.] Albert Shanker, "Where We Stand," September 29, 1991.

coverage in the *New York Times* just as the Milwaukee Parental Choice Program was beginning its third year, and San Antonio CEO was in its first semester. According to Carnegie:

> School choice works better for some parents than for others. Those with *education, sophistication, and especially the right location* may be able to participate in such programs.[64]

A volume called *False Choices: Why School Vouchers Threaten Our Children's Future*, published by Rethinking Schools, the Milwaukee-based anti-voucher organization, and distributed by the National Education Association,[65] serves up the same charge with a rhetorical flourish, calling voucher schools "islands of excellence for the already privileged." How any of these charges square with program requirements that limit voucher eligibility to families at or below the federal free- or reduced-price lunch cutoff—or with the daily experience of choice families in the ghettos and barrios of Cleveland, Milwaukee and San Antonio—is, to put it charitably, difficult to imagine.

Are there any data to support these allegations? Given the Choice experiments begun in the 1990s, we now have accumulated evidence enough to answer a number of questions:

- Are Choice families specially "advantaged," as some school choice critics allege?
- Do Choice programs skim off the "cream of the crop" from urban public schools?
- Where do Choice students come into the program, educationally and behaviorally?

[64.] Carnegie Foundation for the Advancement of Teaching, "School Choice; a Special Report," October 26, 1992, p. 20, emphasis added. For an extended discussion on evaluations of the Milwaukee Choice program, see also Daniel McGroarty, *Break These Chains; the Battle for School Choice*, Prima Publishing (1996), p. 177f.

While the Carnegie Report relies heavily on the research of John Witte—citing his work in 6 of the 13 footnotes in its section on the Milwaukee Choice program—Carnegie chooses not to relay Witte's finding that Milwaukee Parental Choice families' average annual income at that time was $10,700.

[65.] "False Choices: Why School Vouchers Threaten Our Children's Future," *Milwaukee: Rethinking Schools*, Special Issue, September 1992, p. 2.

Recent studies of the Milwaukee, Cleveland, and San Antonio programs provide a statistical snapshot of the typical choice student—and an opportunity to compare that likeness to the claims and charges leveled at choice by its detractors.

FAMILY INCOME

AGAINST A COMMON PROGRAM requirement that participating families must earn no more than the federal free- or reduced-price lunch income levels—$30,433 for a family of four for the 1999-2000 school year—Cleveland choice families are the most "affluent," earning an average $18,750 a year. San Antonio Horizon families earn an average of $15,990 a year—$51 a year more than the $15,939 earned by families with children in the Edgewood public school district.[66] For the Milwaukee choice program, average family income is $10,860—meaning the average choice family could almost triple its income and still officially retain its poverty-stricken status.

Clearly, choice families are among the poorest of the poor, with all of the disadvantages that accompany life far below the poverty line.

FAMILY STATUS

IN MILWAUKEE, STUDIES SHOW that 76 percent of choice students live in single-parent, female-headed households, compared with 65 percent of low-income Milwaukee Public School families.[67] In Cleveland, the percentage of single-parent households is 70 percent.[68] In San Antonio, in contrast to

[66.] Horizon mothers do report somewhat higher levels of employment than their public-school counterparts—50 percent versus 37 percent—and a somewhat lower rate for receiving food stamps (22 percent for Horizon families versus 33 percent for public-school families). Peterson, Myers, Howell, "An Evaluation of the Horizon Scholarship Program," p. 3.

[67.] John F. Witte, Christopher A Thorn, Kim M. Pritchard, and Michele Claibourn, "Fourth Year Report, Milwaukee Parental Choice Program," University of Wisconsin-Madison, December 1994, Table 5c; see also Wisconsin Legislative Audit Bureau Report, 1995, pp. 24-25.

both Milwaukee and Cleveland, 45 percent of Horizon students live with both their mother and father—a percentage, however, that does not differ significantly from the 43 percent of Edgewood ISD students who also live in two-parent families. Again, given the economic and other advantages enjoyed by two-parent families, it is difficult to discern advantage in the family status of the typical choice child.

And yet the claim has been made. University of Wisconsin researcher John Witte, for instance, seized on the fact that Milwaukee Choice families are somewhat smaller, "thus providing an opportunity for parents to focus more on any single child," or as he later put it, permitting a "higher education 'investment' per child."

And in fact, Milwaukee Choice families *are* somewhat smaller than low-income public school families, averaging 2.6 children per family versus 3.24 for low-income MPS families. Once we notice, however, that choice families are overwhelmingly *single-parent*, the putative advantage in parental involvement diminishes, offset by the multiple demands made on a single parent raising two to three children. Based on Witte's own figures, the ratio of children to parents—the only relevant ratio for making inferences about parents concentrating individual attention on each child—narrows to 2.1 children per parent for Choice families, versus 2.4 children per parent for low-income MPS families.[69]

If the Milwaukee data show quite clearly that choice families have precious little money to lavish on their children, a closer look at the numbers also reveals they have precious little time.[70]

[68.] Jay P. Greene, "A Survey of Results from Voucher Experiments: Where We Are and What We Know," March 2000, Table 3.

[69.] John F. Witte, Christopher A Thorn, Kim M. Pritchard, and Michele Claibourn, "Fourth Year Report, Milwaukee Parental Choice Program," University of Wisconsin-Madison, December 1994, Tables 5c and 5d.

[70.] Choice families in Cleveland also have a slightly smaller number of children in the home, 2.6 compared to 2.8 children per family for the average public school family; however, in Cleveland, the preponderance of single-mother households among choice families compared with their public school counterparts is even more pronounced. Peterson, Howell and Greene, "An Evaluation of the Cleveland Voucher Program After Two Years," Harvard Program on Education Policy and Governance, June 1999, Table 1.

MOTHERS' EDUCATIONAL ATTAINMENT

ONE AREA IN WHICH CHOICE FAMILIES do enjoy a measurable advantage is in terms of choice mothers' level of educational attainment. In San Antonio, on average, mothers of Horizon students have completed twelve years of schooling versus eleven years of schooling for public school mothers, while a study of the San Antonio CEO program found that over half of all choice mothers had attended some college, compared to 37 percent of mothers of public school children enrolled in multi-lingual programs and 19 percent of mothers enrolling their children in their public attendance-zone school.[71] In Milwaukee, more than half of all choice mothers—56 percent—reported some college education, compared with 30 percent of all low-income public school mothers.[72] In Cleveland, once again, the same distinction exists: Choice mothers had on average one-year's worth of college courses, while the average mother with public school children was a high school graduate.[73]

Should we reach the common-sense conclusion that a mother's level of education conditions her attitudes towards the importance of education for her children? My answer is a qualified Yes—with a caveat for every interview I have done with mothers whose own experiences as high school dropouts make them even more fiercely committed to their children's academic success.

[71] For the Horizon Program, see Peterson, Myers, Howell, September 1999, p. 2; for San Antonio CEO, see Valerie Martinez, Kenneth Godwin and Frank Kemerer, "Comparing Private and Public School Choice in San Antonio," University of North Texas, January 1995.

[72] John F. Witte, *The Market Approach to Education, An Analysis of America's First Voucher Program*, Princeton University Press, 2000, pp. 59-61, and also see Table 4.2e.

[73] Peterson, Howell and Green, "An Evaluation of the Cleveland Voucher Program After Two Years," Harvard University's Program on Education Policy and Governance, June 1999, p. 6 and Table 1.

STUDENTS' PRIOR ACHIEVEMENT SCORES

WHAT ABOUT THE CHARGE that choice programs are siphoning off the public school's academic high-fliers?

In San Antonio, Jay Greene notes that math scores for incoming choice students are "not statistically different from the average Edgewood [public school] student."[74] Reading scores for incoming Horizon students are higher than their public school peers—35 NPR (national percentile rankings) versus 28 for the average Edgewood student—but both, Greene notes, are very low. 23 percent of Horizon students had been in Gifted and Talented programs at their public school, compared with 29 percent of the overall Edgewood ISD student body,[75] while voucher students and public school students were equally as likely to have been suspended during the past school year.

While prior test scores for all Cleveland choice students are not available, two pieces of evidence suggest that the Cleveland program is attracting less-accomplished public school students. First, Cleveland choice students were about half as likely to have been enrolled in the public school's Gifted and Talented program prior to receiving a voucher—8.4 percent versus 15.2 percent of all public school students. Second, when within weeks of their arrival in the voucher program's first year standardized tests were administered to voucher students at Cleveland's two HOPE Schools—which together enrolled 15 percent of all voucher students and 25 percent of those voucher students who had transferred from public schools[76]—scores ranged from the 31st percentile in math and reading for second through fourth graders, to the 34th and 30th percentiles for math concepts and reading for a second set of

---

[74.] Jay Greene, "A Survey of Results from Voucher Experiments: Where We Are and What We Know," Harvard Program on Education Policy and Governance, March 2000, p. 13. Robert Aguirre, managing director of the Horizon program, notes that baseline tests administered to incoming Choice children showed the average student performing two grade levels below the norm (CEO America Conference, Grand Rapids, Michigan, May 17, 2000).

[75.] Peterson, Myers and Howell, September 1999, p. 16.

[76.] Peterson, Howell and Greene, "An Evaluation of the Cleveland Voucher Program After Two Years," Harvard University's Program on Education Policy and Governance, June 1999, p. 12.

first through fourth grade students.[77] To the extent Cleveland's HOPE schools are epresentative of the program as a whole, Cleveland choice students enter the program well below average in educational achievement.[78]

Shift to Milwaukee, and the statistics tell the same story. Before enrolling in choice schools, Milwaukee students scored at the 31st National Percentile Ranking (NPR) in math and the 29th NPR in reading—significantly below MPS students from other low-income families.[79]

THE CASE AGAINST CREAMING

EVIDENCE SUGGESTS THAT STUDENTS electing to use vouchers are in some instances not measurably different than their public school peers and, in other cases, more likely to be bottom of the barrel than cream of the crop. Even John Witte, the researcher most-quoted by voucher opponents, has indicated:

> [Milwaukee Choice] students were not succeeding in the MPS and probably had higher than average behavioral problems…. In short, the choice students in this program enter very near the bottom in terms of academic achievement.

The students in the Choice Program were not the best, or even average students from the Milwaukee system.[80]

[77.] Greene, Howell, Peterson, "Lessons from the Cleveland Scholarship Program," Harvard University's Program on Education Policy and Governance, December 1997. Table 11.

[78.] Test score comparisons with low-income Cleveland Public School students are hampered by the poor quality of the public school system's test score data, which researcher Jay Greene terms "completely unreliable." (E-mail exchange with the author, August 12, 2000.) For a detailed account of the Cleveland Public Schools data deficiencies, see Paul E. Peterson, Jay P. Greene and William G. Howell, "New Findings from the Cleveland Scholarship Program: A Reanalysis of Data from the Indiana University School of Education Evaluation," Harvard Program on Education Policy and Governance, May 1998, pp. 7-8.

[79.] Witte, John F., *The Market Approach to Education*, Table 4.6, pp. 67-69.

Nor are Witte's findings new. As long ago as his First Year Report, issued in 1991, Witte addressed the "creaming" charge directly— and dismissed it:

> Rather than skimming off the best students, this program seems to provide an alternative educational environment for students who are not doing particularly well in the public school system.[81]

As Jay Greene puts it in his review of eight different evaluations of six existing choice programs[82] by four different research teams:

> Choice does not appear to "cream" the best students. In all studies of existing choice programs the evidence shows that participants have very low family incomes, predominantly come from single-mother households, and have a prior record of low academic performance.[83]

Yet, even as all evidence points to the contrary, voucher opponents are reluctant to abandon their "cream of the crop" charge. Witness Dolores Muñoz, superintendent of the Edgewood public schools—the system under siege from San Antonio's Horizon program—who told a national television audience on Jim Lehrer's "News Hour:"

> I guarantee you that at least 80 percent will be the high-achieving students. The private schools are having the choice of the best students around. . . . Their doors are. . .not open to every child.[84]

[80.] JohnF. Witte, Andrea B. Bailey and Christopher A. Thorn, "Second Year Report, Milwaukee Parental Choice Program," December 1992, p. 8; John F. Witte, "Third Year Report, Milwaukee Parental Choice Program," University of Wisconsin-Madison, December 1993, p. 8; John F. Witte, Christopher A Thorn, Kim M. Pritchard, and Michele Claibourn, "Fourth Year Report, Milwaukee Parental Choice Program," University of Wisconsin-Madison, December 1994, pp. vi and 28.

[81.] John F. Witte, "First Year Report, Milwaukee Parental Choice Program," November 1991, p. iv.

[82.] Milwaukee, Cleveland and San Antonio, plus three additional privately funded voucher programs in New York City, Washington, D.C. and Dayton, Ohio.

[83.] Jay Greene, "A Survey of Results from Voucher Experiments: Where We Are and What We Know," Harvard Program on Education Policy and Governance, March 2000, p. 26

[84.] "Jim Lehrer News Hour," November 27, 1998.

• • •

IN ONE WAY, THE CHOICE students profiled in this book—like many of the choice students I have met over the years—are indeed advantaged, but in a way that carries none of the nefarious connotations choice critics ascribe. They are advantaged by having mothers, fathers or grandparents who are interested and engaged in their schooling, and committed to finding the right school for each child. The question is whether assisting such families—families who are undeniably disadvantaged by so many other measures—is evidence of program defect and policy failure.

About the Author

DANIEL MCGROARTY, Senior Director with the White House Writers Group, a public policy communications consulting firm based in Washington, D.C., is author of *Break These Chains, The Battle for School Choice* (Prima Publishing 1996). His work on education reform and politics has appeared in *The Wall Street Journal, The Los Angeles Times, The Public Interest, National Review, Policy Review,* and *The American Spectator.* Mr. McGroarty served as special assistant to President George H.W. Bush and deputy director of White House speechwriting. He lives with his wife and four children in Chevy Chase, Maryland.